madrid

third edition

Excerpted from *Fodor's Spain*

fodor's travel publications
new york • toronto • london • sydney • auckland

www.fodors.com

contents

maps

on the road with fodor's

A TRIP TAKES YOU OUT OF YOURSELF. Concerns of life at home disappear, driven away by more immediate thoughts—about, say, what marvels will beguile the next day, or where you'll have dinner. That's where Fodor's comes in. We make sure that you know all your options in Madrid, so that you don't miss something that's around the next bend just because you didn't know it was there. Mindful that the best memories of your trip might have nothing to do with what you came to to see, we guide you to sights large and small. With Fodor's at your side, serendipitous discoveries are never far away.

Our success in showing you every corner of Madrid is a credit to our extraordinary writers. They're the kind of people you'd poll for travel advice if you knew them.

Born and educated in Connecticut, writer and journalist **George Semler** has lived in Spain for the last 30-odd years. During that time he has written on Spain, France, Morocco, Cuba, and the Mediterranean region for *Forbes*, *Sky*, *Saveur*, the *International Herald Tribune*, and the *Los Angeles Times* and published walking guides to Madrid and Barcelona. When not hiking, fly-fishing, or sampling Catalonia's hottest new restaurants, he finds time to work on a magnum opus about the Pyrenees.

Writer and editor **AnneLise Sorensen** is currently living in Barcelona, where she's reconnecting with her Catalan roots. Her updating stint took her from the black-sand beaches of the

Canary Islands to the sun-kissed seas of the Costa Blanca and Costa del Sol; from the Roman ruins of Tarragona to the fragrant orange groves of Valencia. AnneLise writes for various magazines and travel publications and has contributed to numerous Fodor's guides, including those to San Francisco, Denmark, and Ireland. She updated Practical Information for this book.

Don't Forget to Write

Your experiences—positive and negative—matter to us. If we have missed or misstated something, we want to hear about it. We follow up on all suggestions. Contact the *Pocket Madrid* editor at editors@fodors.com or c/o Fodor's at 1745 Broadway, New York, New York 10019. And have a fabulous trip!

Karen Cure

Karen Cure
Editorial Director

spain

Ferrol
A Coruña
Vilalba
Ribadeo
Luarca
Gijón
Ribadesella
Bay of Biscay
Santiago de
Compostela
Lugo
Oviedo
Mieres
Cangas
de Onís
Santander
Bilbao
Muros
CANTABRIAN MTS.
PICOS DE
EUROPA
Pontevedra
Ourense
Ponferrada
León
Burgos
Log
Vigo
Astorga
Tui
Benavente
Palencia
Valladolid
Duero
Zamora
Tordesillas
Salamanca
Adanero
Segovia
SIERRA DE GUADARRA
Guadala
Ciudad
Rodrigo
Avila
El Escorial
MADRID
PORTUGAL
SIERRA DE GREDOS
Toledo
Aranjuez
T
Plasencia
Talavera
de la Reina
Alcázar de
San Juan
Tajo
Cáceres
Guadalupe
Trujillo
Mérida
Guadiana
Abenójar
Ciudad
Real
Badajoz
Valdepeñas
Jerez de
los
Caballeros
Zafra
Almadén
Fregenal
de la Sierra
SIERRA MORENA
Bailén
Linares
Ube
Córdoba
Jaén
Baeza
Aroche
Baena
Seville
Gua dalquivir
Ecija
Guadix
Carmona
Lucena
Granada
SIERRA
Huelva
Antequera
Loja
Gulf of
Cádiz
Sanlúcar de
Barrameda
Ronda
Málaga
Nerja
ATLANTIC
OCEAN
Jerez de
la Frontera
Torremolinos
Estepona
Fuengirola
Marbella
Motril
DEL SOL
TO CANARY
ISLANDS
COSTA DE LA LUZ
Cádiz
Algeciras
Gibraltar
COSTA

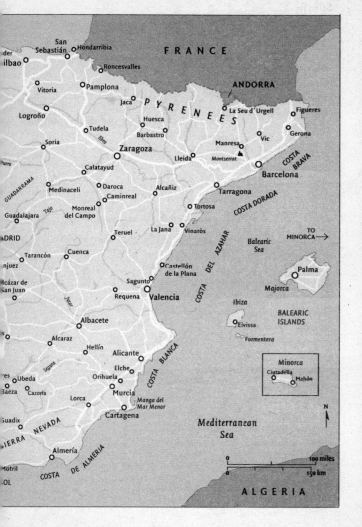

madrid metro

madrid

In This Chapter

introducing madrid

SWASHBUCKLING MADRID CELEBRATES itself and life in general around the clock. After spending much of the 20th century sequestered at the center of a totalitarian regime, Madrid has burst back onto the world stage with an energy redolent of its 16th-century golden age, when painters and playwrights swarmed to the flame of Spain's brilliant royal court. A vibrant crossroads for Iberia and the world's Hispanic peoples and cultures, the Spanish capital has an infectious appetite for art, music, and epicurean pleasure.

After the first gulp of icy mountain air, the next thing likely to strike you is the vast, cerulean, cumulus-clouded sky immortalized in the paintings of Velázquez. "*De Madrid al cielo*" ("from Madrid to heaven") goes the saying, and the heavens seem just overhead at the center of the 2,120-ft-high Castilian plateau. "High, wide, and handsome" might aptly describe this sprawling conglomeration of ancient red-tile rooftops punctuated by redbrick Mudéjar churches and gray-slate roofs and spires left by the 16th-century Habsburg monarchs who made Madrid the capital of Spain in 1561.

And then there are the paintings, the artistic legacy of one of the greatest global empires ever assembled. Having inherited most of Europe by 1506, King Carlos V (1500–58) began to amass art from all corners of his empire, so the early masters of the Flemish, Dutch, Italian, French, German, and Spanish schools found their way to Spain's palaces. The collection was eventually placed in the Prado Museum, part of the grand Madrid built in the 18th century by the Bourbon king Carlos III—known as the Rey-Alcalde, or King-Mayor, for his preoccupation with municipal (rather than global) projects such as the Royal Palace, the Parque del Retiro, and the Paseo del Prado. Among the Prado, the contemporary Reina Sofía museum, the eclectic yet comprehensive Thyssen-Bornemisza collection, and Madrid's smaller artistic repositories—the Real Academia de Bellas Artes de San Fernando, the Convento de las Descalzas Reales, the Sorolla Museum, the Lázaro Galdiano Museum, and still others—there are more paintings in Madrid than anyone can reasonably hope to contemplate in a lifetime.

Modern-day Madrid spreads eastward into the 19th-century grid of the Barrio de Salamanca and sprawls northward through the neighborhoods of Chamberí and Chamartín. But the Madrid to explore carefully on foot is right in the center: the oldest one, between the Royal Palace and Madrid's midtown forest, the Parque del Buen Retiro. These neighborhoods will introduce you to the city's finest resources—its people and their electricity, whether at play in bars or at work in finance or the media and film industries, all in what Madrid's Oscar Wilde, Ramón Gomez de la Serna, called "*la rompeolas de las Españas,*" the breakwater of Spain's many peoples and cultures.

As the highest capital in Europe, Madrid is hot in summer and freezing in winter, with temperate springs and autumns. Especially in winter—when steamy café windows beckon you inside for a hot *caldo* (broth) and the blue skies are particularly bright—Madrid is the next best place to heaven. Moreover, it's ideally placed for cherished getaways to dozens of Castilian hamlets and to Toledo, Segovia, and El Escorial.

PLEASURES AND PASTIMES

Art Museums

Madrid's greatest daytime attractions are its three world-class art museums, the Prado, the Reina Sofía, and the Thyssen-Bornemisza, all within 1 km (½ mi) of each other along the leafy

Paseo del Prado, sometimes called the Paseo del Arte. The Prado has the world's foremost collections of Goya, El Greco, and Velázquez, topping off hundreds of other 14th- to 19th-century masterpieces. The Reina Sofía focuses on modern art, especially Dalí, Miró, and Picasso, whose famous *Guernica* hangs here; it also shows contemporary Spanish artists, such as Jorge Oteiza, Eduardo Chillida, Antoni Tàpies, and Antonio Lopez, as well as postmodern temporary exhibits. The Thyssen-Bornemisza encompasses the entire history of Western art, with collections of impressionist and German expressionist works.

Bullfighting

Bullfighting is an artistic spectacle, not to be confused with sport. For those not squeamish about the sight of six dying bulls every Sunday afternoon from April to early November, it offers all the excitement of a major stadium event. Nowhere in the world is bullfighting better than at Madrid's Las Ventas—formally the Plaza de Toros Monumental—on Calle Alcalá in Salamanca. The sophisticated audience follows taurine matters closely, and the uninitiated might be baffled by their reactions: cheers and hoots can be hard to distinguish, and it can take years to understand what prompts the wrath of such a hard-to-please crowd. Tickets can be purchased at the ring or, for a 20% surcharge, at one of the agencies on Calle Victoria, just off the Puerta del Sol. Most *corridas* start in late afternoon, and the best fights of all—the world's top displays of bullfighting—come during the three weeks of consecutive daily events that mark the feast of San Isidro, in May.

Music

Madrid's musical offerings range from Bach organ recitals in the Catedral de la Almudena to flamenco performances with dinner at Casa Patas. In between there are world-class groups playing in intimate chapels, churches and convents, the Auditori Nacional, the Teatro Real opera house, the auditorium at the Academia Real de Bellas Artes de San Fernando, and an always interesting list of concert venues. Ongoing is a classical series organized by the Juan March Foundation. Architecture is never better appreciated than when set to music; check listings for musical events held in often-unvisitable spaces.

Tapas Bars

Next to paintings, Madrid's tapas may be the city's most creative and irresistible attraction. Originally a lid used to *tapar* (cover or close) a glass of wine, a *tapa* is a bit of food that often comes free with a drink; it might be a few olives, a mussel in vinaigrette, a sardine, or spicy potatoes. A larger serving, called *una ración*, is also available. The best place to start a tapa tour is in and around Plaza Santa Ana or in the *mesones* built into the wall beneath the Plaza Mayor, along Cava de San Miguel. Each bar here specializes in a different tapa—for example, the omeletlike potato-and-egg *tortilla* (not to be confused with the Mexican tortilla), garlicky mushrooms, manchego cheese, or plates of *jamón ibérico*.

QUICK TOURS

Tour One

If you have only a day or two, limit yourself to a couple museums and devote the rest of your time to wandering. See the works of Spain's great masters at the **MUSEO DEL PRADO**; then visit the **PALACIO REAL** for a regal display of art, architecture, and history. The palace tour includes admission to the Royal Library and Royal Armory, both sights in their own right. Stroll from Paseo de la Castellana to Paseo del Prado to see the fountains at **PLAZA COLÓN: FUENTE DE LA CIBELES** and **FUENTE DE NEPTUNO**. Behold the **PUERTA DEL SOL**, then relax at an outdoor café on the **PLAZA MAYOR**. Finally, pop into some of the historic tapas bars along **CAVA DE SAN MIGUEL**.

Tour Two

With three or four days you can uncover historic Madrid, visit more museums, and make an excursion outside the city. Follow the two-day plan above; then visit the **CENTRO DE ARTE REINA SOFÍA** and the **MUSEO THYSSEN-BORNEMISZA**. Try not to miss the 16th-century **CONVENTO DE LAS DESCALZAS REALES**. Explore the Mudéjar architecture and flamboyant plateresque decoration of medieval Madrid in the **PLAZA DE LA VILLA** and around the **PLAZA DE LA PAJA**. Venture outside the capital to spend your fourth day at **EL ESCORIAL**, a grand monastery, or **CHINCHÓN**, a true Castillian village.

In This Chapter

Updated by George Semler

here and there

THE REAL MADRID IS NOT TO BE FOUND along its major arteries such as Gran Vía and the Paseo de la Castellana. To find the quiet, intimate streets and squares that give the city its true character, duck into the warren of villagelike byways in the downtown area 2½ km (1½ mi) square extending from the Royal Palace to the Parque del Retiro and from Plaza de Lavapiés to the Glorieta de Bilbao. Broad *avenidas*, twisting medieval alleys, grand museums, stately gardens, and tiny, tiled taverns are all jumbled together, creating an urban texture so rich that walking is really the only way to soak it in. Sadly, petty street crime has become a serious problem in Madrid, and tourists are frequent targets. Be on your guard, and try to blend in: wear dark clothes, keep cameras concealed, and avoid flamboyant map reading. The Japanese embassy has complained to Madrid authorities that tourists who appear East Asian seem to be at particular risk.

Numbers in the text correspond to numbers in the margin and on the Exploring Madrid map.

GREAT ITINERARIES

If You Have 2 Days

Harvest the highlights of the major art museums and devote the rest of your time to wandering. On the first morning, see the masterworks in the **MUSEO DEL PRADO** ㉑ and tour the Paseo del Prado between Atocha train station and **PLAZA COLÓN** ㉟, past the fountains at **FUENTE DE NEPTUNO** ⑳ and the **PLAZA DE LA CIBELES** ㉙. Walk up past the Westin Palace and have lunch in

exploring madrid

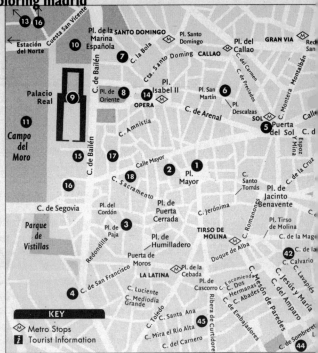

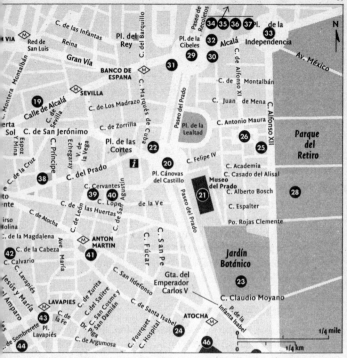

or near **PLAZA SANTA ANA** ㊳; then cut through the **PUERTA DEL SOL** ⑤ for a look at Madrid's Times Square on your way to the **PLAZA MAYOR** ①. Cut behind the glass-and-iron Mercado de San Miguel and through tiny Calle Puñonrostro to **PLAZA DE LA VILLA** ⑱ on your way to the church of **SAN NÍCOLAS DE LAS SERVITAS** ⑰ and then the **PLAZA DE ORIENTE** ⑧, where you might want to tour the **PALACIO REAL** ⑨ and/or the **TEATRO REAL** ⑭. If it's summer, take in the sunset from a terrace table at El Ventorrillo at the south end of Calle Bailén's Viaducto. Later, visit the tapas bars along **CAVA DE SAN MIGUEL** ②, dine at Botín or Casa Paco, and walk home through **PLAZA MAYOR** ①.

On day two, see Picasso's *Guernica* and the works of Miró and Dalí at the **CENTRO DE ARTE REINA SOFÍA** ㉔. Have lunch in one of the many eateries on Cava Baja, in Lavapiés. Walk through the **PLAZA DE LA PAJA** ③, Plaza Mayor, and Plaza Santa Ana before exploring the **MUSEO THYSSEN-BORNEMISZA** ㉒ for an overview of Western art. Take a sunset stroll in the Parque del Buen Retiro before dinner.

If You Have 4 Days

In four days you can uncover historic Madrid, spend more time with the paintings, and make an excursion outside the city. Follow the two-day plan above; then, on day three, taxi or hike up the Paseo de la Castellana to the **MUSEO SOROLLA** ㊱ and the **MUSEO LÁZARO GALDIANO** ㊲ for more memorable paintings. Take in the 16th-century **CONVENTO DE LAS DESCALZAS REALES** ⑥ and the **CONVENTO DE LA ENCARNACIÓN** ⑦ on your way, perhaps, to the restaurant La Bola. Drive or take a train out of Madrid for your third night and fourth day in **TOLEDO** or **SEGOVIA**.

OLD MADRID

The narrow streets of old Madrid wind back through the city's history to its beginnings as an Arab fortress. Madrid's historic quarters are not so readily apparent as the ancient neighborhoods of Toledo and Segovia, nor are they so grand, but make time to explore their quiet, winding alleys.

A Good Walk

Start in the **PLAZA MAYOR** ①. Looking up at the playfully erotic mural on the Casa de la Panadería (Bakery House, named for its former role as Madrid's medieval bread dispensary), exit under the arch to the far left and walk down Ciudad Rodrigo; then turn left. Across the street is the restored San Miguel market; down **CAVA DE SAN MIGUEL** ② are tapas bars that reach into caves under Plaza Mayor. The entrance to Las Cuevas de Luis Candelas is on the left, by the steps up to the Plaza Mayor. As Cava de San Miguel becomes Calle Cuchilleros, Botín is on the left, Madrid's oldest restaurant and a onetime Hemingway haunt. Curvy Cuchilleros was once a moat just outside the city walls.

The plaza with the bright murals at the intersection of Calle Segovia is called **Puerta Cerrada,** or Closed Gate, for the (always closed) city gate that once stood here. The mural up to the left reads, "*Fui sobre agua edificada; mis muros de fuego son*" ("I was built on water; my walls are made of fire"), a reference to the city's origins as a fortress with abundant springs and its ramparts made of silex, the kind of flint that creates sparks. Across the square to the right is Calle del Nuncio, leading to the Palacio de la Nunciatura (Palace of the Nunciat), which once housed the Pope's ambassadors to Spain. The palace isn't open, but you can peek inside the Renaissance garden.

Nuncio widens and on your left at No. 17 is the Taberna de Cien Vinos; sample some Spanish wine there. Opposite is the church of San Pedro el Viejo (St. Peter the Elder), one of Madrid's oldest, with a Mudéjar tower. Bear right and enter Príncipe Anglona to enter **PLAZA DE LA PAJA** ③. Down on the right is the ramped Costanilla de San Andrés, which leads to Calle Segovia and a view of the viaduct above. Look down the narrow Calle Príncipe Anglona to see the Mudéjar tower on the church of San Pedro.

The brick tower was reportedly built in 1354 following the Christian reconquest of Algeciras, near Gibraltar.

At the top of Plaza de la Paja is the church of San Andrés; past the church, turn right after Plaza de los Carros into Plaza Puerta de Moros, then down Carrera San Francisco to visit the **BASÍLICA DE SAN FRANCISCO EL GRANDE** ④. Backtrack and turn left after San Andrés down Cava Baja, packed with bars and restaurants. Casa Lucio, at No. 35, is said to be a favorite of King Juan Carlos I; La Chata at No. 24, is a typical Madrid *tasca* (tavern) with spectacular ceramic tilework on the facade. Julián de Tolosa at No. 18 has fine Basque fare. Continue across Puerta Cerrada and up Calle Cuchilleros to return to Plaza Mayor.

TIMING

This two-hour walk requires some short uphill climbs through the winding streets. Allow ample time for stops to absorb some café and terrace life—especially in summer, when heat will be a factor.

Sights to See

④ **BASÍLICA DE SAN FRANCISCO EL GRANDE.** In 1760, Carlos III built this impressive basilica on the site of a Franciscan convent, allegedly founded by St. Francis of Assisi in 1217. The dome, 108 ft in diameter, is the largest in Spain, even larger than that of St. Paul's in London, where its 19 bells were cast in 1882. The seven main doors were carved of American walnut by Casa Juan Guas. Three chapels adjoin the circular church, the most famous being that of **San Bernardino de Siena,** which contains a Goya masterpiece depicting a preaching San Bernardino. The figure standing on the right, not looking up, is a self-portrait of Goya. The 16th-century Gothic choir stalls came from La Cartuja del Paular, in rural Segovia province. *Pl. de San Francisco, Lavapiés, tel. 91/365–3400. Free. Tues.–Fri. 11–12:30 and 4–6:30.*

★ ② **CAVA DE SAN MIGUEL.** The narrow, picturesque streets behind the Plaza de la Villa are well worth exploring: from Plaza Mayor, turn onto Plaza de San Miguel, with the glass-and-iron Mercado de San Miguel (St. Michael's Market) on your right. Stroll down Cava de San Miguel past the row of **ancient tapas bars** built into the retaining wall of Plaza Mayor above. Each one specializes in a different delicacy: Mesón de Champiñones (mushrooms), Mesón de Boquerónes (anchovies), Mesón de Tortilla (Spanish potato omelet), and so on. About halfway down the street is one of Madrid's oldest taverns, **Las Cuevas de Luis Candelas,** named for a romantic, Robin Hood–like, 19th-century Madrid bandit. *Behind Plaza de la Villa, Cava de San Miguel.*

NEED A BREAK? The **CAFÉ DEL NUNCIO** (Costanilla del Nuncio s/n, Plaza Mayor), on the corner of Calle Segovia, is a relaxing place for a coffee or beer against a backdrop of classical music.

❸ **PLAZA DE LA PAJA.** At the top of the hill, on Costanilla San Andrés, the Plaza de la Paja was the most important square in medieval Madrid. The plaza's jewel is the **Capilla del Obispo** (Bishop's Chapel), built between 1520 and 1530; this was where peasants deposited their tithes, called *diezmas*—literally, one-tenth of their crop. The stacks of wheat on the chapel's ceramic tiles refer to this tradition. Architecturally, the chapel marks a transition from the blockish Gothic period, which gave the structure its basic shape, to the Renaissance, the source of the decorations. Go inside to see the intricately carved polychrome altarpiece by Francisco Giralta, with scenes from the life of Christ. Opening hours are erratic; try to visit during mass or on feast days. The chapel is part of the complex of the domed church of **San Andrés,** built for the remains of Madrid's male patron saint, San Isidro Labrador. Isidro was a peasant who worked fields belonging to the Vargas family. The 16th-century **Vargas palace** forms the eastern side of the Plaza de la Paja. According to legend, St. Isidro worked little but had the best-tended fields thanks to many hours of prayer. When Señor Vargas came out to investigate the phenomenon, Isidro made a spring of sweet water spurt from the ground to quench his master's thirst. Because St. Isidro's power had to do with water, his remains were traditionally paraded through the city in times of drought. *Plaza de la Paja, Centro.*

❶ PLAZA MAYOR. Austere, grand, and often surprisingly quiet compared to the rest of Madrid, this arcaded square has seen it all: autos-da-fé (trials of faith, i.e., public burnings of heretics); the canonization of saints; criminal executions; royal marriages, such as that of Princess María and the King of Hungary in 1629; bullfights (until 1847); masked balls; fireworks; and all manner of other events and celebrations. It still hosts fairs, bazaars, and performances.

Measuring 360 ft by 300 ft, Madrid's Plaza Mayor is one of the largest and grandest public squares in Europe. It was designed by Juan de Herrera, the architect to Felipe II and designer of the El Escorial monastery, northwest of Madrid. Construction of the plaza lasted just two years and was finished in 1620 under Felipe III, whose equestrian statue stands in the center. The inauguration ceremonies included the canonization of four Spanish saints: Teresa of Ávila, Ignatius of Loyola, Isidro (Madrid's male patron saint), and Francis Xavier.

This space was once occupied by a city market, and many of the surrounding streets retain the names of the trades and foodstuffs once headquartered there. Nearby are Calle de Cuchilleros (Knifemakers' Street), Calle de Lechuga (Lettuce Street), Calle de Fresa (Strawberry Street), and Calle de Botoneros (Buttonmakers' Street). The plaza's oldest building is the one with the brightly painted murals and the gray spires, called Casa de la Panadería (Bakery House) in honor of the bread shop over which it was built. Opposite is the Casa de la Carnicería (Butcher Shop), now a police station.

The plaza is closed to motorized traffic, making it a pleasant place to sit at one of the sidewalk cafés, watching alfresco artists, street musicians, and Madrileños from all walks of life. Sunday morning brings a stamp and coin market. Around Christmas the plaza fills with stalls selling trees, ornaments, and nativity scenes, as well as all types of practical jokes and tricks for December 28, Día de los Inocentes—a Spanish version of April Fool's Day. *Plaza Mayor, Centro.*

CENTRAL MADRID

The 1-km (½-mi) stretch between the Royal Palace and the Puerta del Sol is loaded with historic sites.

A Good Walk

Begin at the **PUERTA DEL SOL** ⑤, the center of Madrid. If you stand with your back to the clock, Calle Arenal is the second street from the far left leaving the plaza: walk down Arenal and turn right into Plaza Celenque. Up on your left, at the corner with Calle Misericordia, is the **CONVENTO DE LAS DESCALZAS REALES** ⑥. Follow Misericordia and turn left into the charming Plaza de San Martín to return to Calle Arenal. Turn right and walk down to Plaza Isabel II; then cross the plaza to your right and walk to the end of the short Calle de Arrieta, at which point you'll face the **CONVENTO DE LA ENCARNACIÓN** ⑦. Turn left here into Calle Pavia (off Calle San Quintin) and you'll enter the **PLAZA DE ORIENTE** ⑧.

Here you have a choice of going directly to the **PALACIO REAL** ⑨, to your right, or visiting its gardens (1 km [½ mi] farther on) and/or taking a cable-car ride. For the latter, cross Calle Bailén and walk to the right: you'll have a view across the formal **JARDINES SABATINI** ⑩ to the Casa de Campo park and the Guadarrama Mountains. Walk up Bailén, avoiding the overpass, and turn left down Cuesta de San Vicente, then left into Paseo Virgin del Puerto for the entrance to the gardens and the **CAMPO DEL MORO** ⑪. To see the Egyptian **TEMPLO DE DEBOD** ⑫, cross the overpass to Calle Ferraz and follow the Parque del Oeste on the left. Farther along Paseo de Pintor Rosales, in the park, is the **TELEFÉRICO** ⑬ (cable car) to the Casa de Campo, which grants panoramic views of Madrid. Opposite the Royal Palace on the Plaza de Oriente is the **TEATRO REAL** ⑭. Walking down Bailén with the palace on your right, you can enter its huge courtyard and admire the view from atop the escarpment. Alongside the palace is the **CATEDRAL DE LA ALMUDENA** ⑮. Walk past the cathedral and turn right onto Calle Mayor: on your left, on Cuesta de la Vega, are the remains of Madrid's **ARAB WALL** ⑯.

Walk back east up Calle Mayor, crossing Bailén. Turn left onto Calle San Nicolás to see the church of **SAN NICOLÁS DE LOS SERVITAS** ⑰. Return to Calle Mayor and press ahead: on your right you'll see the **PLAZA DE LA VILLA** ⑱, with Madrid's city hall on the right. Farther up Mayor, bear right on Plaza Morenas and enter the **PLAZA MAYOR** ① through the arch. The Andalusian Torre de Oro bar on the left displays gory pictures of bullfights, not for the squeamish. On the far side, at No. 33, is the restaurant El Soportal, which gives the plaza's best free tapas with each drink order. (Beware of prices at the other restaurants, especially if you sit outside.) Exit the plaza to the left of El Soportal and head down Calle de Postas and back to the Puerta del Sol. Proceed up the right side of Sol, past the headquarters of the regional government, and in winter consider having a traditional *caldo* (broth) in the charming old shop at the restaurant Lhardy on Carrera de San Jerónimo.

TIMING
Without side trips to the palace gardens or the cable car, you can cover this ground in two hours. Set aside an additional morning or afternoon to visit the Royal Palace.

Sights to See

⑯ **ARAB WALL.** The remains of the Moorish military outpost that became the city of Madrid are visible on Calle Cuesta de la Vega. The sections of wall here protected a fortress built in the 9th century by Emir Mohammed I. In addition to being an excellent defensive position, the site had plentiful water and was called

Mayrit, Arabic for "source of life" and the likely origin of the city's name. All that remains of the *medina*—the old Arab city that formed within the walls of the fortress—is the neighborhood's crazy quilt of streets and plazas, which probably follow the same layout they followed more than 1,100 years ago. The park **Emir Mohammed I,** alongside the wall, hosts concerts and plays in the summer. *C. Cuesta de la Vega, Centro.*

⑪ **CAMPO DEL MORO** (Moors' Field). Below the Sabatini Gardens, but accessible only by an entrance on the far side, is the Campo del Moro. Enjoy the clusters of shady trees, winding paths, and the long lawn leading up to the Royal Palace. Even without considering the riches inside, the palace's immense size (it's twice as large as Buckingham Palace) inspires awe. *Paseo Virgen del Puerto s/n, Centro.*

⑮ **CATEDRAL DE LA ALMUDENA.** The first stone of the cathedral (which adjoins the Royal Palace to the south) was laid in 1883 by King Alfonso XII, and the end result was consecrated by Pope John Paul II in 1993. The building was intended to be Gothic in style, with needles and spires, but funds ran low, the design was simplified by Fernando Chueca Goltia into the existing, more austere classical form. The cathedral has the remains of Madrid's patron saint, San Isidro (St. Isidore), and a wooden statue of Madrid's female patron saint, the Virgin of Almudena, reportedly discovered after the 1085 Christian reconquest of Madrid. Legend has it that a divinely inspired woman named María led authorities to a grain storage vault (in Arabic, *almudeyna*) in the old wall of the Alcázar, now part of the cathedral's foundation, where the statue was found framed by two lighted candles. *C. Bailén s/n, Barrio de Oriente, tel. 91/548–9900. Free. Daily 10–1:30 and 6–7:45.*

⑦ **CONVENTO DE LA ENCARNACIÓN** (Convent of the Incarnation). Once connected to the Royal Palace by an underground passageway, this Augustinian convent was founded in 1611 by the wife of Felipe III. It has several artistic treasures, including a reliquary, which holds among the sacred bones a vial containing the dried blood of St. Pantaleón, which is said to liquefy every year on July 27. The ornate church has superb acoustics for medieval and Renaissance choral music; check city listings for concerts. *Plaza de la Encarnación 1, Opera, tel. 91/547–0510. €3. Wed. and Sat. 10:30–2:30 and 4–5:30, Sun. 11–2.*

⑥ CONVENTO DE LAS DESCALZAS REALES (Convent of the Royal Discalced, or Barefoot, Nuns). This 16th-century building was restricted for 200 years to women of royal blood. Its plain, brick-and-stone facade hides paintings by Zurbarán, Titian, and Brueghel the Elder, as well as a hall of sumptuous tapestries crafted from drawings by Peter Paul Rubens. The convent was founded in 1559 by Juana of Austria, whose daughter shut herself up here rather than endure marriage to Felipe II. A handful of nuns (not necessarily royal) still live here, cultivating their own vegetables in the convent's garden. The required tour is conducted only in Spanish. *Plaza de las Descalzas Reales 3, Centro, tel. 91/521–2779. €5. Tues.–Thurs. and Sat. 10:30–12:45 and 4–5:45, Fri. 10:30–12:45, Sun. 11–1:45.*

⑩ JARDINES SABATINI (Sabatini Gardens). The formal gardens to the north of the Royal Palace are crawling with stray cats, but they're a pleasant place to rest or watch the sun set. *C. Bailén s/n, Centro.*

★ ⑨ PALACIO REAL. The Royal Palace was commissioned in the early 18th century by the first of Spain's Bourbon rulers, Felipe V, on the same strategic site where Madrid's first Alcázar (Moorish fortress) was built in the 9th. Before you enter, admire the classical French architecture on the graceful **Patio de Armas.** King Felipe was obviously inspired by his childhood days at Versailles with his grandfather Louis XIV. Look for the stone statues of Inca prince Atahualpa and Aztec king Montezuma, perhaps the only tributes in Spain to these pre-Columbian American rulers. Notice how the steep bluff drops westward to the Manzanares River—on a clear day, this vantage point also commands a view of the mountain passes leading into Madrid from Old Castile, and you'll see why the Moors picked this particular spot for a fortress.

Inside, 2,800 rooms compete with each other for over-the-top opulence. A nearly two-hour guided tour in English winds a mile-long path through the palace. Highlights include the **Salón de Gasparini,** King Carlos III's private apartments, with swirling, inlaid floors and curlicued, ceramic wall and ceiling decoration, all glistening in the light of a 2-ton crystal chandelier; the **Salón del Trono,** a grand throne room with the royal seats of King Juan Carlos and Queen Sofía; and the **banquet hall,** the palace's largest room, which seats up to 140 people for state dinners. No monarch has lived here since 1931, when Alfonso XIII was deposed following a republican electoral victory. The current king and queen live in the far simpler Zarzuela Palace on the outskirts of Madrid, using this palace only for official occasions.

Also visit the **Biblioteca Real** (Royal Library), with a first edition of Cervantes's *Don Quixote;* the **Museo de Música** (Music Museum), where five stringed instruments by Stradivarius form the world's largest collection; the **Armería Real** (Royal Armory), with historic suits of armor and frightening medieval torture implements; and the **Real Oficina de Farmacía** (Royal Pharmacy), with vials and flasks used to mix the king's medicines. *C. Bailén s/n, Centro, tel. 91/542–0059. €6, guided tour €7. Apr.–Sept., Tues.–Sat. 9–6, Sun. 9–3; Oct.–Mar., Tues.–Sat. 9:30–5, Sun. 9:30–2. Closed during official receptions.*

8 PLAZA DE ORIENTE. The stately plaza in front of the Royal Palace is surrounded by massive stone statues of various Spanish monarchs from Ataulfo to Fernando VI. These sculptures were meant to be mounted on the railing on top of the palace, but Queen Isabel of Farnesio, one of the first royals to live in the palace, had them removed because she was afraid their enormous weight would bring the roof down. (Well, that's what she *said* . . . according to palace insiders, the queen wanted the statues removed because her own likeness had not been placed front and center.) The statue of **King Felipe IV** in the plaza's center was the first equestrian bronze ever cast with a rearing horse.

The pose comes from a Velázquez painting of the king with which the monarch was so smitten that in 1641 he commissioned an Italian artist, Pietro de Tacca, to turn it into a sculpture. De Tacca enlisted Galileo's help in configuring the statue's weight so it wouldn't tip over. For most Madrileños, the Plaza de Oriente is forever linked with Francisco Franco. The *generalísimo* liked to speak from the roof of the Royal Palace to his followers as they crammed into the plaza below. Even now, on the November anniversary of Franco's death, the plaza fills with supporters, most of whom are old-timers, though the event occasionally has drawn swastika-waving skinheads from other European countries in a chilling fascist tribute. *Plaza de Oriente, Centro.*

⑱ PLAZA DE LA VILLA. Madrid's town council has met in this medieval-looking complex since the Middle Ages, and it's now the city hall. Just two blocks west of the Plaza Mayor on Calle Mayor, it was once called Plaza de San Salvador for a church that used to stand here. The oldest building is the **Casa de los Lujanes,** on the east side—it's the one with the Mudéjar tower. Built as a private home in the late 15th century, the house carries the Lujanes crest over the main doorway. Also on the plaza's east end is the brick-and-stone **Casa de la Villa,** built in 1629, a classic example of Madrid design with its clean lines and spire-topped corner towers. Connected by an overhead walkway, the **Casa de Cisneros** was commissioned in 1537 by the nephew of Cardinal Cisneros. It's one of Madrid's rare examples of the Flamboyant Plateresque style, which has been likened to splashed water—a liquid exuberance wrought in stone. *C. Mayor, Centro. Guided tour in Spanish Mon. at 5.*

⑤ PUERTA DEL SOL. Crowded with people and exhaust, Sol is the nerve center of Madrid's traffic. The city's main subway interchange is below, and buses fan out from here. A brass plaque in the sidewalk on the south side of the plaza marks Kilometer 0, the spot from which all distances in Spain are measured. The restored 1756 French-neoclassical building near the marker now houses the offices of the regional government, but during Franco's reign it was the headquarters of his secret police, and it's still known folklorically as the Casa de los Gritos (House of Screams). Across the square is a bronze statue of Madrid's official symbol, a bear with a *madroño* (strawberry tree), and a statue of King-Mayor Carlos III on horseback. *Puerta del Sol, Centro.*

⑰ SAN NICOLÁS DE LAS SERVITAS (Church of St. Nicholas of the Servitas). This church tower is one of the oldest buildings in Madrid. There is some debate over whether it once formed part of an Arab mosque. It was more likely built after the Christian reconquest of Madrid in 1085, but the brickwork and the horseshoe arches are evidence that it was crafted by either Moorish workers (Mudéjars) or Spaniards well versed in the style. Inside, exhibits detail the Islamic history of early Madrid. *Near Plaza de San Nicolás, Centro, tel. 91/559–4064. Donation suggested. Tues.–Sun. 6:30 AM–8:30 PM or by appointment.*

⑭ TEATRO REAL (Royal Theater). Built in 1850, this neoclassical theater was long a cultural center for Madrileño society. A major restoration project has left it replete with golden balconies, plush seats, and state-of-the-art stage equipment for operas and ballets. *Plaza de Isabel II, Centro, tel. 91/516–0660, www.teatro-real.com.*

⑬ TELEFÉRICO. Kids love this cable car, which takes you from just above the Rosaleda gardens in the Parque del Oeste to the center of Casa de Campo. Be warned that the walk from where the cable car drops you off to the zoo and the amusement park is at least 2 km (1 mi), and you'll have to ask directions; it's easier to ride out, turn around, and come back. *Estación Terminal Teleférico, Jardines Rosaleda (at C. Marques de Urquijo), Centro, tel. 91/541–7450. €3. Apr.–Sept., daily noon–dusk; Oct.–Mar., weekends noon–3 and 4–6.*

⑫ TEMPLO DE DEBOD. This authentic 4th-century BC Egyptian temple was donated to Spain in gratitude for its technical assistance with the construction of the Aswan Dam. It's near the site of the former Montaña barracks, where Madrileños bloodily crushed the beginnings of a military uprising in 1936. *Hill in Parque de la Montaña, near Estación del Norte, Centro, tel. 91/765–1008.*

€2, free Wed. and Sun. Oct.–Mar., Tues.–Fri. 10–1:30 and 4:30–6, weekends 10–1:30; Apr.–Sept., Tues.–Fri. 4:30–7:45, weekends 10–1:30.

THE ART WALK

Madrid's three art museums are all within walking distance of one another via the Paseo del Prado. The Paseo was designed by King-Mayor Carlos III as a leafy nature walk with glorious fountains and a botanical garden for respite in scorching summers. As you walk east down Carrera de San Jerónimo toward the Paseo del Prado, consider that this was the route followed by Ferdinand and Isabella more than 500 years ago toward the church of San Jerónimo el Real.

A Good Walk

Exit the **PUERTA DEL SOL** ⑤ onto Calle de Alcalá, and you'll find on your left the **REAL ACADEMIA DE BELLAS ARTES DE SAN FERNANDO** ⑲. Take the next right, past the elegant bank buildings, onto Calle Sevilla and turn left at Plaza Canalejas— where La Violeta, at No. 6, sells violet-flavor sweets—onto Carrera de San Jerónimo. (If you cross the plaza onto Calle Príncipe, you'll reach the Plaza Santa Ana tapas area.) Walk down San Jerónimo to Plaza de las Cortés.

The granite building on the left, its stairs guarded by bronze lions, is the Congreso, lower house of Las Cortés, Spain's parliament. Walk past the landmark Westin Palace on the right to the **FUENTE DE NEPTUNO** ⑳ in the wide Paseo del Prado— the **MUSEO DEL PRADO** ㉑ is across the boulevard to the right. On your left is the **MUSEO THYSSEN-BORNEMISZA** ㉒, and across the plaza on the left is the elegant Ritz hotel, alongside the obelisk dedicated to all those who have died for Spain. Either tackle one or both of these museums now, or continue strolling.

Turning right and walking south on Paseo del Prado, you'll see the **JARDÍN BOTÁNICO** ㉓ on the left and eventually **ESTACIÓN**

DE ATOCHA ㊻, a railway station said to resemble the overturned hull of a ship. It's worth a quick visit for its humid indoor park with tropical trees, benches, paths, and a restaurant. Across the traffic circle, the immense pile of painted tiles and winged statues houses Spain's Ministry of Agriculture. The **CENTRO DE ARTE REINA SOFÍA** ㉔, site of Picasso's *Guernica*, is in the building with the exterior glass elevators, best accessed by walking up Calle Atocha from the station and taking the first left. Retracing your steps to the Fuente de Neptuno, turn right and walk between the Ritz and the Prado. Straight ahead you'll see the **CASÓN DEL BUEN RETIRO** ㉕, on its left the **MUSEO DEL EJÉRCITO** ㉖, and farther on the cloister of the church of **SAN JERÓNIMO EL REAL** ㉗ and the vast **PARQUE DEL RETIRO** ㉘.

Back at the fountain again, turn left and walk up the left side of Paseo del Prado (or, even better, the leafy central promenade) past the Museo Thyssen-Bornemisza to the **PLAZA DE LA CIBELES** ㉙, surrounded by the **PALACIO DE COMUNICACIONES** ㉚, the **BANCO DE ESPAÑA** ㉛, and the **CASA DE AMÉRICA** ㉜. Turn right at Cibeles, walk up Calle Alcalá, and you'll see Madrid's unofficial symbol: the **PUERTA DE ALCALÁ** ㉝, and, again, the Parque del Retiro. About 100 yards north of Cibeles, on the Paseo de Recoletos, you'll see a grand yellow mansion on the right—now a bank headquarters, this was once the home of the Marquis of Salamanca, who at the turn of the 20th century built the exclusive shopping and residential neighborhood (northeast of here) that now bears his name. Continue north for the **MUSEO ARQUEOLÓGICO** ㉞, which adjoins the National Library, and the **PLAZA COLÓN** ㉟. If you're an art buff, press on to the **MUSEO SOROLLA** ㊱ and **MUSEO LÁZARO GALDIANO** ㊲.

TIMING
With a visit to the Reina Sofía and the Parque del Retiro, you can do this walk in three to four hours. Set aside a morning or an afternoon *each* to return to the Prado and Thyssen-Bornemisza.

Sights to See

③① BANCO DE ESPAÑA. This massive 1884 building, Spain's central bank, takes up an entire block. It is said that the nation's gold reserves are held in great vaults that stretch under the Plaza de la Cibeles' traffic circle all the way to the fountain. The bank is not open to visitors, but if you can dodge traffic well enough to reach the median strip in front of it, you can take a fine photo of the fountain and the palaces with the Puerta de Alcalá arch in the background. *Paseo del Prado s/n, at Plaza de la Cibeles, Centro.*

③② CASA DE AMÉRICA. A cultural center and art gallery focusing on Latin America, the Casa is in the allegedly haunted Palacio de Linares, built by a man who made his fortune in the New World and returned to a life of incestuous love and strange deaths. *Paseo de Recoletos 2, Centro, tel. 91/595–4800. Free. Tues.–Fri. 11–8, Sat. 11–7, Sun. 11–2.*

②⑤ CASÓN DEL BUEN RETIRO. This Prado annex is just a five-minute walk from the museum and is free with a Prado ticket. The building, once a ballroom, and the formal gardens in the Retiro are all that remain of Madrid's second royal complex, which filled the entire neighborhood until the early 19th century. On display are 19th-century Spanish paintings and sculpture, including works by Sorolla and Rusiñol. A regal restoration of the complex will yield brand-new halls devoted to 17th- and 19th-century Spanish art. *C. Alfonso XII s/n, Retiro, tel. 91/330–2867. Tues.–Sat. 9–7, Sun. 9–2.*

★ **②④ CENTRO DE ARTE REINA SOFÍA** (Queen Sofía Art Center). Madrid's museum of modern art is in a converted hospital whose classical granite austerity is somewhat relieved (or ruined, depending on your point of view) by the playful pair of glass elevator shafts on its facade. The collection focuses on Spain's three great modern masters—Pablo Picasso, Salvador Dalí, and Joan Miró—and has contributions from Juan Gris, Jorge Oteiza, Pablo Gargallo, Julio Gonzalez, Eduardo Chillida, and Antoni Tàpies. Take the elevator to the second floor to see the heavy hitters, then to the fourth floor for the rest of the permanent collection, which includes both Spanish and international artists. The other floors have traveling exhibits. The exhibition rooms are numbered 1–45, beginning chronologically with the turn-of-the-20th-century birth of Spain's modern movement on the second floor and continuing to contemporary artists such as Eduardo Chillida in Rooms 42 and 43 on the fourth floor. The free English-language guide-booklet is excellent, as are the plastic-covered notes available at each display.

The museum's showpiece is Picasso's *Guernica,* in the center hall on the second floor. Surrounded by studies for its many individual elements, the huge black-and-white canvas depicts the horror of the Nazi Condor Legion's bombing of the ancient Basque town of Guernica in 1937, during the Spanish Civil War. The work—in tone and structure a 20th-century version of Goya's The 3rd of May—is something of a national shrine. *Guernica* did not reach Madrid until 1981, as Picasso had stipulated in his will that the painting only return to Spain after democracy was restored.

The room in front of *Guernica* has **surrealist** works, with six canvases by Miró. Room 10 belongs to Salvador Dalí hung in three *ámbitos* (areas). The first has the young artist experimenting with different styles, as in his cubist self-portrait and his classical landscape Paisaje de Cadaqués; the second shows the evolving painter of the Buñuel portrait and portraits of the artist's sister; and the third includes the full-blown surrealist work for which Dalí is best known, The Great Masturbator (1929) and The Enigma of Hitler (1939), with its broken, dripping telephone.

The rest of the museum is devoted to more recent art, including the massive sculpture Toki Egin, by Eduardo Chillida, considered Spain's greatest living sculptor, and five paintings by Barcelona artist Antoni Tàpies, whose works use such materials as wrinkled sheets and straw. Santa Isabel 52, Atocha, tel. 91/467–5062. €3, free Sat. after 2:30 and all day Sun. Mon. and Wed.–Sat. 10–9, Sun. 10–2:30.

46 **ESTACIÓN DE ATOCHA.** Madrid's Atocha railroad station, a steel-and-glass hangar, was built in the late 19th century by Alberto Palacio Elissague, the same architect who became famous for his work with Ricardo Velázquez in the creation of the Palacio de Cristal (Crystal Palace) in Madrid's Retiro park. The immense space was filled in the late 20th century with a tropical rain forest. For many years closed, and nearly torn down during the '70s, Atocha was restored and refurbished by Spain's internationally acclaimed architect Rafael Moneo. *Paseo de Atocha s/n, Retiro, tel. 91/420–9875.*

20 **FUENTE DE NEPTUNO** (Neptune's Fountain). At Plaza Canovas del Castillo, midway between the Palace and Ritz hotels and the Prado and Thyssen-Bornemisza museums, this fountain is at the hub of Madrid's Paseo del Arte. It was a rallying point for Atlético de Madrid soccer triumphs (counterpoint to Real Madrid's celebrations at the Fuente de la Cibeles up the street). It's been quiet here for the past few years, with Atlético mired in second division (a concept comparable to the New York Mets' slipping down to the minors). With Atlético's return to first division in spring of 2002, the Fuente de Neptuno reassumed its pivotal role in Madrid life. *Plaza Canovas del Castillo, Centro.*

23 **JARDÍN BOTÁNICO** (Botanical Garden). Just south of the Prado Museum, the gardens provide a pleasant place to stroll or sit under the trees. True to the wishes of King Carlos III, they hold many plants, flowers, and cacti from around the world. *Plaza de Murillo 2, Retiro, tel. 91/420–3017. €1.5. Summer, daily 10–9; winter, daily 10–6.*

34 **MUSEO ARQUEOLÓGICO** (Museum of Archaeology). The museum shares its neoclassical building with the **Biblioteca Nacional** (National Library). The biggest attraction here is a replica of the prehistoric cave paintings in Altamira, Cantabria, located underground in the garden. (Access to the real thing is highly restricted.) Inside the museum, look for *La Dama de Elche,* a bust of a wealthy, 5th-century BC Iberian woman, and notice that her headgear is a rough precursor to the mantillas and hair combs still associated with traditional Spanish dress. The ancient Visigothic votive crowns are another highlight, discovered in 1859 near Toledo and believed to date back to the 8th century. *C. Serrano 13, Salamanca, tel. 91/577–7912. €3, free Sat. after 2:30 and all day Sun. Museum Tues.–Sat. 9:30–8:30, Sun. 9:30–2:30; reproduction cave paintings Tues.–Sat. 11–2:30 and 5:30–6:30, Sun. 11–2:30.*

㉖ MUSEO DEL EJÉRCITO (Army Museum). A real treat for arms-and-armor buffs, this place is right on the museum mile. Among the 27,000 items on view are a sword that allegedly belonged to the Spanish hero El Cid; suits of armor; bizarre-looking pistols with barrels capable of holding scores of bullets; Moorish tents; and a cross carried by Christopher Columbus. It's an unusually entertaining collection. *Mendez Nuñez 1, Retiro, tel. 91/522–8977. €1. Tues.–Sun. 10–2.*

★ **㉑ MUSEO DEL PRADO** (Prado Museum). When the Prado was commissioned by King-Mayor Carlos III, in 1785, it was meant to be a natural-science museum. The king wanted the museum, the adjoining botanical gardens, and the elegant Paseo del Prado to serve as a center of scientific enlightenment. By the time the building was completed in 1819, its purpose had changed to exhibiting the art gathered by Spanish royalty since the time of Ferdinand and Isabella. The museum is adding a massive new wing, designed by Rafael Moneo, that will resurrect long-hidden works by Zurbarán and Pereda and more than double the number of paintings on display from the permanent collection.

The Prado's jewels are its works by the nation's three great masters: Francisco Goya, Diego Velázquez, and El Greco. The museum also holds masterpieces by Flemish, Dutch, German, French, and Italian artists, collected when their lands were part of the Spanish Empire. The museum benefited greatly from the anticlerical laws of 1836, which forced monasteries, convents, and churches to forfeit many of their artworks for public display.

Enter the Prado via the Goya entrance, with steps opposite the Ritz hotel, or by the less-crowded Murillo door opposite the Jardín

Botánico. The layout varies (grab a floor plan), but the first halls on the left, coming from the Goya entrance (7A to 11 on the second floor, or *planta primera*), are usually devoted to **17th-century Flemish painters,** including Peter Paul Rubens (1577–1640), Jacob Jordaens (1593–1678), and Antony van Dyck (1599–1641).

Room 12 introduces you to the meticulous brushwork of **Velázquez** (1599–1660) in his numerous portraits of kings and queens. Look for the magnificent *Las Hilanderas* (The Spinners), evidence of the artist's talent for painting light. The Prado's most famous canvas, Velázquez's *Las Meninas* (The Maids of Honor), combines a self-portrait of the artist at work with a mirror reflection of the king and queen in a revolutionary interplay of space and perspectives. Picasso was obsessed with this work and painted several copies of it in his own abstract style, now on display in the Picasso Museum in Barcelona.

The south ends of the second and top floors (*planta primera* and *planta segunda*) are reserved for **Goya** (1746–1828), whose works span a staggering range of tone, from bucolic to horrific. Among his early masterpieces are portraits of the family of King Carlos IV, for whom he was court painter—one glance at their unflattering and imbecilic expressions, especially in the painting *The Family of Carlos IV*, reveals the loathing Goya developed for these self-indulgent, reactionary rulers. His famous side-by-side canvases, *The Clothed Maja* and *The Nude Maja*, may represent the young duchess of Alba, whom Goya adored and frequently painted. No one knows whether she ever returned his affection. The adjacent rooms house a series of idyllic scenes of Spaniards at play, painted as designs for tapestries.

Goya's paintings took on political purpose starting in 1808, when the population of Madrid rose up against occupying French troops. *The 2nd of May* portrays the insurrection at the Puerta del Sol, and its even more terrifying companion piece, *The 3rd of May*, depicts the nighttime executions of patriots who had rebelled the day before. The garish light effects in this work typify the romantic style, which favors drama over detail, and make it one of the most powerful indictments of violence ever committed to canvas.

Goya's "black paintings" are dark, disturbing works, completed late in his life, that reflect his inner turmoil after losing his hearing and his deep embitterment over the bloody War of Independence. These are copies of the monstrous hallucinatory paintings Goya made with marvelously free brush strokes on the walls of his house by southern Madrid's Manzanares River, popularly known as *La Quinta del Sordo* (the deaf one's villa). Having grown gravely ill in his old age, Goya was deaf, lonely, bitter, and despairing; his terrifying *Saturn Devouring One of his Sons* communicates the ravages of age and time.

Near the Goya entrance, the Prado's ground floor (*planta baja*) is filled with 15th- and 16th-century Flemish paintings, including the bizarre pre-surrealist masterpiece *Garden of Earthly Delights*, by Hieronymous Bosch (c. 1450–1516). Next come Rooms 60A, 61A, and 62A, filled with the passionately spiritual works of **El Greco** (Doménikos Theotokópoulos, 1541–1614), the Greek-born artist who lived and worked in Toledo. El Greco is known for his mystical, elongated forms and faces. His style was quite shocking to a public accustomed to strictly representational images. Two of his greatest paintings, *The Resurrection* and *The Adoration of the Shepherds*, are on view here. Before you leave, stop in the 14th- to 16th-century Italian rooms to see Titian's *Portrait of Emperor Charles V* and Raphael's exquisite *Portrait of a Cardinal*. *Paseo del Prado s/n, Retiro, tel. 91/420–3768, www.museoprado.mcu.es. €3, free Sat. after 2:30 and all day Sun. Tues.–Sat. 9–7, Sun. 9–2.*

NEED A BREAK? **LA DOLORES** (Plaza de Jesús 4, Santa Ana) is an atmospheric old ceramic-tile bar that's the perfect place for a beer or glass of wine and a plate of olives. It's a great alternative to the Prado's basement cafeteria and is just across the Paseo, then one block up on Calle Lope de Vega.

③ MUSEO LÁZARO GALDIANO. A 10-minute walk across the Castellana from the Museo Sorolla, the stately mansion of writer and editor José Lázaro Galdiano (1862–1947) is an abrupt change of pace from the cozy Bohemian intimacy of Sorolla's house. With both decorative items and paintings by Bosch, El Greco, Murillo, and Goya, among others, this is a remarkable collection of five centuries of Spanish, Flemish, English, and Italian art. Bosch's *St. John the Baptist* and the many Goyas are the stars of the show, with El Greco's *San Francisco de Assisi* and Zurbarán's *San Diego de Alcalá* close behind. *Serrano 122, Salamanca, tel. 91/561–6084. €3. Tues.–Sun. 10–2.*

③ MUSEO SOROLLA. Spain's most famous impressionist painter, Joaquín Sorolla (1863–1923), lived and worked here for most of his life. Entering this diminutive but cozy domain is a little like stepping into a Sorolla painting, as it's filled with the artist's best-known works, most of which shimmer with the bright Mediterranean light and color of his native Valencia. Because the house and garden were also designed by Sorolla, you leave with an impression of the world as seen through this painter's exceptional eye. *General Martínez Campos 37, Chamberí, tel. 91/310–1584. €3. Tues.–Sat. 10–3, Sun. 10–2.*

② MUSEO THYSSEN-BORNEMISZA. The newest of Madrid's three major art centers, the "Thyssen" occupies spacious galleries washed in salmon pink and filled with natural light in the late-18th-century Villahermosa Palace, finished in 1771. This ambitious collection of 800 paintings traces the history of Western art with examples from every important movement, from the 13th-century Italian Gothic through 20th-century American Pop Art. The works were gathered from the 1920s to the 1980s by Swiss industrialist Baron Hans Heinrich Thyssen-Bornemisza and his father. At the urging of his wife, Carmen Cervera (a former Miss Spain), the baron donated the entire collection to Spain in 1993. Critics have described these paintings as the minor works of major artists and the major works of minor artists, but, be that as it may, the collection traces the development of Western humanism as no other in the world.

One of the high points here is Hans Holbein's *Portrait of Henry VIII* (purchased from the late Princess Diana's grandfather, who used the money to buy a new Bugatti sports car). American artists are also well represented; look for the Gilbert Stuart portrait of George Washington's cook, and note how closely the composition and rendering resemble the artist's famous painting of the Founding Father himself. Two halls are devoted to the Impressionists and Postimpressionists, including many works by Pissarro and a few each by Renoir, Monet, Degas, van Gogh, and Cézanne. Find Pissarro's *Saint-Honoré Street in the Afternoon, Effect of Rain* for a jolt of mortality, or Renoir's *Woman with a Parasol in a Garden* for a sense of bucolic beauty lost. Picasso's *Harlequin with a Mirror* is a self-portrait of a spurned (by Sara Murphy, it is said) lover, while Dalí's *Dream Caused by the Flight of a Bee Around a Pomegranate a Second before Awakening* will take you back to Hieronymous Bosch's *Garden of Earthly Delights*, 300 yards and half a millennium away in the Prado.

Within 20th-century art, the collection is strong on dynamic and colorful German expressionism, with some soothing works by Georgia O'Keeffe and Andrew Wyeth along with Hoppers, Bacons, Rauschenbergs, and Lichtensteins. Last but not least, the temporary exhibits are often fascinating. *Paseo del Prado 8, Centro, tel. 91/369–0151, www.museothyssen.org. €5. Tues.–Sun. 10–7.*

㉚ PALACIO DE COMUNICACIONES. This ornate building on the southeast side of Plaza de la Cibeles is Madrid's main post office. *Plaza de Cibeles, Centro, tel. 902/197197. Stamps weekdays 9 AM–10 PM, Sat. 9–8, Sun. 10–1; phone, telegrams, and fax weekdays 8 AM– midnight, weekends 8 AM–10 PM.*

★ ☝ ㉘ **PARQUE DEL RETIRO** (literally, the Retreat). Once the private playground of royalty, Madrid's crowning park is a vast expanse of green encompassing formal gardens, fountains, lakes, exhibition halls, children's play areas, outdoor cafés, and a **Puppet Theater,** featuring free slapstick routines that even non–Spanish speakers will enjoy. Shows take place on Saturday at 1 and on Sunday at 1, 6, and 7. The park is especially lively on weekends, when it fills with street musicians, jugglers, clowns, gypsy fortune-tellers, and sidewalk painters along with hundreds of Spanish families out for a walk. The park hosts a book fair in May and occasional flamenco concerts in summer. From the entrance at the Puerta de Alcalá, head straight toward the center and you'll find the **Estanque** (lake), presided over by a grandiose equestrian statue of King Alfonso XII, erected by his mother. Just behind the lake, north of the statue, is one of the best of the park's many cafés. If you're feeling nautical, you can rent a boat and work up an appetite rowing around the lake.

The 19th-century **Palacio de Cristal** (Crystal Palace), southeast of the Estanque, was built to house exotic plants from the Philippines, a Spanish possession at the time. This airy marvel of steel and glass sits on a base of decorative tile. Next door is a small lake with ducks and swans. At the south end of the park, along the Paseo del Uruguay, is the **Rosaleda** (rose garden), an English garden bursting with color and heavy with floral scents for most of the summer. West of the Rosaleda, look for a statue called the **Ángel Caído** (Fallen Angel), which Madrileños claim is the only one in the world depicting the prince of darkness before (during, actually) his fall from grace. *Puerta de Alcalá, Retiro.*

35 PLAZA COLÓN. Named for Christopher Columbus, this plaza has a statue of the explorer (identical to the one in Barcelona's port) looking west from a high tower in the middle of the square. Beneath the plaza is the **Centro Cultural de la Villa** (tel. 91/575–6080), a performing-arts facility. Behind Plaza Colón is **Calle Serrano,** the city's premier shopping street (think Gucci, Prada, and Loewe). Stroll in either direction on Serrano for some window-shopping. *Plaza Colón, Centro.*

EL ESPEJO (Paseo de Recoletos 31, Centro) comprises two classy bars near the Plaza Colón—one in a Belle Epoque setting on a side street, the other in a pavilion of glass and wrought iron in the middle of the Paseo de Recoletos. Sit on the shady terrace or in the air-conditioned, stained-glass bar and rest your feet while sipping a coffee or a beer.

㉙ PLAZA DE LA CIBELES. A tree-lined walkway runs down the center of Paseo del Prado to the grand Plaza de la Cibeles, where the famous Fuente de la Cibeles (Fountain of Cybele) depicts the nature goddess driving a chariot drawn by lions. Even more than the officially designated bear and arbutus tree, this monument, beautifully lighted at night, has come to symbolize Madrid—so much so that during the civil war, patriotic Madrileños risked life and limb to sandbag it as Nationalist aircraft bombed the city. *Plaza de la Cibeles, Centro.*

㉝ PUERTA DE ALCALÁ. This triumphal arch was built by Carlos III in 1778 to mark the site of one of the ancient city gates. You can still see the bomb damage inflicted on the arch during the civil war. *C. de Alcalá s/n, Retiro.*

⑲ REAL ACADEMIA DE BELLAS ARTES DE SAN FERNANDO (St. Ferdinand Royal Academy of Fine Arts). Designed by Churriguera in the waning baroque years of the early 18th century, this little-known museum showcases 500 years of Spanish painting, from Ribera and Murillo to Sorolla and Zuloaga. The tapestries along the stairways are stunning. The same building houses the **Instituto de Calcografía** (Prints Institute), which sells limited-edition prints from original plates engraved by Spanish artists, including Goya. Check listings for classical and contemporary concerts in the small upstairs concert hall. *Alcalá 13, Sol, tel. 91/522–0046. €3, free Wed. Tues.–Fri. 9:30–7, Sat.–Mon. 9–2:30.*

㉗ SAN JERÓNIMO EL REAL. Ferdinand and Isabella used this church and cloister as a *retiro*, or place of meditation—hence the name of the nearby park. The building was devastated in the Napoléonic Wars, then rebuilt in the late 19th century. *Moreto 4, behind Prado museum, Retiro, tel.* 91/420–3578. *Daily* 8–1:30 *and* 5:30–8:30.

CASTIZO MADRID

The Spanish word *castizo* means "authentic," and *los Madrileños castizos* are the Spanish equivalent of London's cockneys. There are few "sights" in the usual sense on this route; instead, you wander through some of Madrid's most traditional and lively neighborhoods. Within these are a growing number of immigrants and the attendant employment problems. Purse-snatching and petty crime are not uncommon, so think twice about this walk if you don't feel streetwise.

A Good Walk

Begin at the **PLAZA SANTA ANA** ㊳, hub of the theater district in the 17th century and now a center of nocturnal activity, not all of it desirable. The plaza's notable buildings include, at the lower end, the Teatro Español. Walk up to the sunny Plaza del Ángel (next to the Reina Victoria hotel) and turn down Calle de Las Huertas, past the ancient olive tree and plant nursery behind the San Sebastián church—once the church cemetery, this was the final resting place for poets such as Lope de Vega and Quevedo. Walk down Huertas to No. 18, Casa Alberto, an ancient (still excellent) bar and restaurant as well as the house where Miguel de Cervantes was living when he finished his last novel, *Viaje al Parnaso*. Continue to Calle León, named for a lion kept here long ago by a resident Moor. A short walk to your left brings you past the González delicatessen and bar to the corner of Calle Cervantes. As the plaque on the wall overhead attests, *Don Quixote's* author died on April 23, 1616, in what is now called the **CASA DE CERVANTES** ㊴. Down the street, at No. 11, is the **CASA DE LOPE DE VEGA** ㊵, where the "Spanish Shakespeare," Fray Felix Lope de Vega Carpio, lived and worked.

A right from Calle Cervantes onto Calle Quevedo takes you past the Basque *sidrería* (cider house) Zerain—where you can catch cider in your glass as it spurts directly from the barrel—down to the corner across from the convent and church of the Trinitarias Descalzas (Discalced, or Barefoot, Trinitarians, a cloistered order of nuns). Miguel de Cervantes is buried inside with his wife and daughter. Turn right on Calle Lope de Vega to return to Calle León, and walk left back to Calle Huertas. One block to the left on Huertas, turn right onto Calle Amor de Dios and walk to its end, the busy Calle Atocha; across the street is the church of San Nicolás. The predecessor of this plain, modern church was burned in 1936, but the site is historic: like many churches during that turbulent period, the original building fell to the wrath of working-class crowds who felt victimized by centuries of clerical oppression. To the left of the church, walk down Pasaje Doré, where, if it's early in the day, you'll pass through the Anton Martín market, a colorful assortment of stalls typical of most Madrid neighborhoods.

Turn right on Calle Santa Isabel, by the **CINE DORÉ** ㊶, and take your first left on Calle de la Rosa, which after a jog to the right becomes Calle de la Cabeza. You'll pass the restaurant Casa Lastra. On the southwest corner with Calle Lavapiés is the site of the **CÁRCEL DE LA INQUISICIÓN** ㊷. Turn left here: this is the beginning of the Barrio Lavapiés, Madrid's old Judería (Jewish Quarter). Like Moors, Jews were forced to live outside the city walls after the Christian reconquest hit Madrid in 1085, and this was one of the suburbs they founded. Known as Lavapiés (literally, "washfeet") after the medieval custom of bathing one's feet before entering the *aljama* (ghetto), this hillside neighborhood is a quintessentially grass-roots working-class Madrid barrio, rife with artists, students, and aspiring actors, though gentrification is beginning to creep in; the streets have been recobbled, and lighting improved. Holding your belongings tightly and your camera out of sight, explore side streets off Calle Lavapiés; then continue down and south until you reach the heart of the neighborhood, **PLAZA LAVAPIÉS** ㊸.

Leave the plaza heading west on Calle Sombrerete. After two blocks you'll reach the intersection of Calle Mesón de Paredes, on which corner you'll see a lovingly preserved example of a popular Madrid architecture, the **CORRALA** ㊹. Life in this type of balconied apartment building is very public, with laundry flapping in the breeze, babies crying, and old women gossiping over the railings. Neighbors once shared common kitchen and bath facilities on the patio. Work your way west, crossing Calle de Embajadores into the neighborhood known as **EL RASTRO** ㊺, with streets of small family stores selling furniture, antiques, and a cornucopia of used junk (some of it greatly overpriced). On Sunday, El Rastro becomes a flea market, and Calle de Ribera de Curtidores, the steep main drag, is closed to traffic and jammed with outdoor booths, shoppers, and pickpockets.

TIMING

Allow at least three hours. The Anton Martín market comes to life every weekday morning, while the streets surrounding the Plaza Santa Ana are more interesting after dark, as they pack some of Madrid's best tapas bars and nightspots. El Rastro can be saved for a Sunday morning if you decide to join the milling throng at the flea market.

Sights to See

㊷ **CÁRCEL DE LA INQUISICIÓN** (Inquisition Jail). Unmarked by any historical plaque, the former jail is now a large tapas bar, the **Taberna del Avapiés,** named for the old Jewish Quarter. Here Jews, Moors, and others designated unrepentant heathens or sinners bent to the inquisitors' whims; the prison later became a Cárcel de la Corona (Crown Prison) for the incarceration of wayward soldiers, priests, and nuns. Ask a bartender if you can see the original, two-story medieval patio out back—it's tiny, but highly

evocative. *Southeast corner of C. Cabeza and C. Lavapiés, Lavapiés, tel.
91/369–3218. Daily 9 AM–2 AM.*

39 **CASA DE CERVANTES.** A plaque marks the private home where Miguel de Cervantes Saavedra, author of *Don Quixote de la Mancha*, committed his final words to paper: "*Puesto ya el pie en el estribo, con ansias de la muerte . . .*" ("One foot already in the stirrup and yearning for death . . ."). The Western world's first runaway best-seller, and still one of the most widely translated and read books in the world, Cervantes' spoof of a knightly novel playfully but profoundly satirized Spain's rise and decline while portraying man's dual nature in the pragmatic Sancho Panza and the idealistic Don Quixote, ever in search of wrongs to right. *C. Cervantes and C. León, Santa Ana.*

40 **CASA DE LOPE DE VEGA.** Considered the Shakespeare of Spanish literature, Fray Felix Lope de Vega Carpio (1562–1635), a contemporary and adversary of Cervantes, wrote some 1,800 plays and enjoyed great success during his lifetime. His former home is now a museum with period furnishings, offering an intimate look into a bygone era: everything here, from the whale-oil lamps and candles to the well in the tiny garden and the pans used to warm the bedsheets, brings you closer to the great dramatist. Don't miss the Latin inscription over the door: PARVA PROPIA MAGNA / MAGNA ALIENA PARVA (small but mine big / big but someone else's small). *C. Cervantes 11, Santa Ana, tel. 91/429–9216. €2. Sept.–July, weekdays 9:30–2, Sat. 10–2.*

NEED A
BREAK? **TABERNA DE ANTONIO SÁNCHEZ** – Drop into Madrid's oldest tavern for a glass of wine and some tapas, or just a peek. The dark walls (lined with bullfighting paintings), zinc bar, and pulley system used to lift casks of wine from the cellar look much the same as they did when the place first opened in 1830. Meals are also served in a dining room in the back. Specialties include *rabo de buey* (bull's-tail stew) and *morcillo al horno* (beef stew). *Mesón de Paredes 13, Lavapiés.*

④① CINE DORÉ. A rare example of art nouveau architecture in Madrid, the hip Cine Doré shows movies from the Spanish National Film Archives and eclectic foreign films. Show times are listed in newspapers under "*Filmoteca*." The lobby, trimmed with smart pink neon, has a sleek café-bar and a good bookshop. *C. Santa Isabel 3, Lavapiés, tel. 91/369–1125. Tues.–Sun.; hrs vary depending on show times.*

④④ CORRALA. This structure is not unlike the rowdy outdoor areas, known as *corrales*, used as Madrid's early makeshift theaters; they were usually installed in a vacant lot between two apartment buildings, and families with balconies overlooking the action rented out seats to wealthy patrons of the arts. There's a plaque here to remind you that the setting for the famous 19th-century *zarzuela* (light opera) *La Revoltosa* was a corrala like this one. City-sponsored musical-theater events are occasionally held here in summer. The ruins across the street were once the **Escolapíos de San Fernando,** one of several churches and parochial schools that fell victim to anti-Catholic sentiments during the civil war. *C. Mesón de Paredes and C. Sombrerete, Lavapiés.*

④⑤ EL RASTRO. Named for the *arrastre* (dragging) of animals in and out of the slaughterhouse that once stood here and, specifically, the *rastro* (blood trail) left behind, this site explodes into a rollicking flea market every Sunday morning from 10 to 2. For serious browsing and bargaining, any *other* morning is a better time to turn up treasures such as old iron grillwork, a marble tabletop, or a gilt picture frame, but Sundays bring out truly bizarre bric-a-brac ranging from stolen earrings to sent postcards to thrown-out love letters. Even so, people-watching is the best part. *Ribera de los Curtidores s/n, Centro.*

④③ PLAZA LAVAPIÉS. The heart of the historic Jewish barrio, this plaza remains a neighborhood hub. To the left is the Calle de la Fe (Street of Faith), which was called Calle Sinagoga until the expulsion of the Jews in 1492. The church of **San Lorenzo** at the end was built on the site of the razed synagogue. Legend has it that Jews and Moors who chose baptism over exile were forced to walk up this street barefoot to the ceremony to demonstrate their new faith. *Top of C. de la Fe, Lavapiés.*

38 **PLAZA SANTA ANA.** This plaza was the heart of the theater district in the 17th century—the golden age of Spanish literature—and is now the center of Madrid's thumping nightlife. A statue of 17th-century playwright Pedro Calderón de la Barca faces the **Teatro Español.** Rebuilt in 1980 following a fire, the theater stands on the site where plays were performed as early as the 16th century in a corrala. Opposite the theater, the **Casa de Guadalajara,** with a facade of ceramic tile, is a popular nightspot. The **Gran Hotel Reina Victoria** was not always so upscale but has always been favored by bullfighters, including Manolete. Off to the side of the hotel is the diminutive **Plaza del Ángel,** with one of Madrid's best jazz clubs, the Café Central. Back on Plaza Santa Ana is one of Madrid's most famous cafés, the former Hemingway hangout **Cervecería Alemana,** still catnip to writers, poets, and beer drinkers. *Plaza de Santa Ana s/n, Centro.*

Updated by George Semler

eating out

MADRID HAS ATTRACTED GENERATIONS OF COURTIERS, diplomats, and tradesmen, all of whom have brought tastes and styles from other parts of the Iberian peninsula and the world. The city's best restaurants have traditionally specialized in Basque cooking, though contemporary Mediterranean interpretations from Catalonia and even Asian fusion restaurants have begun to rock the city's culinary canons. Madrid's many seafood specialists capitalize on the abundant fresh produce trucked in nightly from the Atlantic and the Mediterranean coasts.

Madrid's own cuisine is based on the roasts and thick soups and stews of Castile, Spain's high central *meseta* (plain). Roast suckling pig and lamb are standard Madrid feasts, as are baby goat and chunks of beef from Ávila. *Cocido madrileño* and *callos a la madrileña* are local specialties. Cocido is a hearty winter meal of broth, garbanzo beans, vegetables, potatoes, sausages, pork, and hen. The best cocidos are simmered in earthenware crocks over coals and served in three courses: broth, beans, and meat. Cocido anchors the midday winter menu in the most elegant restaurants as well as the humblest holes-in-the-wall. Callos are a simpler concoction of veal tripe stewed with tomatoes, onions, hot paprika, and garlic. *Jamón serrano* (cured ham)—a specialty from the livestock lands of Teruel, Extremadura, and Andalusia—has become a Madrid staple; wanderers are likely to come across a *museo del jamón* (literally, ham museum), where legs of the dried delicacy dangle in store windows or in bars. For top-quality free-range, acorn-fed, native Iberian ham ask for *jamón ibérico de bellota*.

For faster dining, try *bocadillo de tortilla* (potato omelet sandwich) or a *cazuelita* (small earthenware bowl) of anything from wild mushrooms to *riñones al jerez* (lamb or veal kidneys stewed in sherry).

The house wine in basic Madrid restaurants is often a sturdy, uncomplicated Valdepeñas from La Mancha. Serious dining is normally accompanied by a Rioja or a more powerful, complex Ribera de Duero, the latter from northern Castile. Ask your waiter's advice; a smooth Rioja, for example, may not be up to the task of accompanying a cocido or a roast suckling pig. After-dinner, try the anise-flavor liqueur (*anís*) produced outside the nearby village of Chinchón.

Madrileños tend to eat their meals even later than in other parts of Spain, and that's saying something. There are just too many exciting things to do each day (including work) to get around to the final stanza any sooner than necessary. Restaurants open for lunch at 1:30 and fill up by 3, during which time most offer a *menú del día* (daily fixed-price special) comprising main course, wine, dessert, and coffee. Dinnertime begins at 9, but reservations for 11 are common, and a meal can be a wonderfully lengthy (up to three hours) affair. Don't fight it; a late dinner here is the only kind. If you face hunger meltdown several hours before dinner, make the most of the early evening tapas hour.

Prices and Dress

Dress in most Madrid restaurants and tapas bars is casual but stylish. Compared with Barcelona, the pricier places are a bit more formal; men often wear jackets and ties, and women often wear skirts.

CATEGORY	COST*
$$$$	over €24
$$$	€18–€24
$$	€12–€18
$	under €12

*per person for a main course at dinner

$$$–$$$$ HORCHER. Once Madrid's best restaurant, this classic at the edge of the Retiro is now widely considered little more than an overpriced reminder of its former glory. Nevertheless, the Horcher faithful continue to fill this shrine to fine dining. Wild boar, venison, and roast duck are standard fare, while lobster salad with truffles is a star appetizer. Stroganoff with mustard, pork chops with sauerkraut, and *baumkuchen* (a chocolate-covered fruit and cake dessert) reflect the restaurant's Germanic roots. The intimate dining room is decorated with rust-color brocade and antique Austrian porcelain; an ample selection of French and German wines rounds out the menu. Jacket and tie are required. *Alfonso XII 6, Retiro, tel. 91/522–0731. Reservations essential. AE, DC, MC, V. Closed Sun. and Aug. No lunch Sat.*

$$$–$$$$ LA BROCHE. Sergi Arola, a Ferrán Adriá disciple, has vaulted
★ directly to the apex of Madrid dining. The minimalist dining room allows you to concentrate on the hot-cold, surf-turf counterpoints of your codfish soup with bacon ice cream or marinated sardine with herring roe. The *menú de degustación* permits Sergi and his staff to run you through the gastronomic color wheel, generally progressing from light to dark, fish to foie, seafood to tenderloin. Try a peppery Priorat (a Miserere, for example) with your beef or venison. *Miguel Angel 29, Chamberí, tel. 91/399–3778. Reservations essential. AE, DC, MC, V. Closed Sun. and 1 wk at Easter. No lunch Sat.*

$$$–$$$$ LA TERRAZA—CASINO DE MADRID. This rooftop terrace just
★ off Puerta del Sol is in one of Madrid's oldest, most exclusive clubs (the *casino*, a club for gentlemen, not gamblers). The food is inspired and overseen by Ferrán Adriá, who runs his own famous restaurant, El Bullí, near Roses in Catalonia. Francisco Roncero's

creations closely follow Adriá's trademarks: the lightest and tastiest of mousses and foams, ravioli in rare flavors that explode in the mouth, or *crustaceos en suquet con alcachofas y patatas* (crustaceans with artichokes and potatoes). Try the 11-plate tasting menu. *Alcalá 15, Sol, tel. 91/521–8700. Reservations essential. AE, DC, MC, V. Closed Sun. and Aug. No lunch Sat.*

$$$–$$$$ LHARDY. Serving Madrid specialties for more than 150 years, Lhardy looks about the same as it must have on day one, with its dark-wood paneling, brass chandeliers, and red-velvet chairs. Most people come for the traditional *cocido a la madrileña* and *callos a la madrileña*. Game, sea bass, and soufflés are also available. Dining rooms are upstairs; the ground-floor entry doubles as a delicatessen and stand-up coffee bar that fills on chilly winter mornings with shivering souls sipping steaming-hot *caldo* (broth) from silver urns. *Carrera de San Jerónimo 8, Sol, tel. 91/522–2207. AE, DC, MC, V. Closed Aug. No dinner Sun.*

$$$–$$$$ SANTCELONI. Santi Santamaria's Madrid branch of his Racó de Can Fabes just outside of Barcelona has proved an immediate and major success in the Spanish capital. Along with Juan Mari Arzak and Ferrán Adriá, one of the reigning troika of Spanish chefs, Santamaria may be the best of all. Lighter and more original than Arzak, less playful and bizarre than Adriá, Santamaria serves up exquisite combinations of Mediterranean ingredients accompanied by a comprehensive and daring wine list. *Paseo de la Castellana 57, Chamberí, tel. 91/210–8840. Reservations essential. AE, DC, MC, V. Closed Sun. and Aug. No lunch Sat.*

$$$–$$$$ VIRIDIANA. Viridiana has a relaxed, somewhat cramped bistro feel, its black-and-white scheme punctuated by prints from Luis Buñuel's classic anticlerical film (for which the place is named). Iconoclast chef Abraham Garcia says "market-based" is too narrow a description for his creative menu, which changes every two weeks with the season. Look for red onions stuffed with *morcilla* (black pudding); soft flour tortillas wrapped around marinated fresh tuna; or filet mignon in white truffle sauce. Try the superb duck pâté drizzled with sherry and served with Sauternes or Tokay wine. *Juan de Mena 14, Retiro, tel. 91/531–5222. Reservations essential. AE, DC, MC, V. Closed Sun. and Holy Week.*

$$$–$$$$ **ZALACAÍN.** A deep-apricot color scheme, set off by dark wood and ★ gleaming silver, calls to mind an exclusive villa. Zalacaín introduced nouvelle Basque cuisine to Spain in the 1970s and is now a Madrid classic. Splurge on dishes like prawn salad in avocado vinaigrette, lobster salad in an emulsion of virgin olive oil and sherry vinegar, and roast pheasant with truffles; or sample the chef's tasting menu. Service is somewhat stuffy, and jackets and ties are required. *Alvarez de Baena 4, Chamartín, tel. 91/561–4840. Reservations essential. AE, DC, V. Closed Sun., Aug., and 1 wk at Easter. No lunch Sat.*

$$–$$$$ **ASADOR FRONTÓN I.** Fine meat and fish are the headliners here. Uptown, Asador Frontón II is swankier, but this downtown original is more charming. Appetizers include *anchoa fresca* (fresh grilled anchovies) and *pimientos rellenos con bacalao* (peppers stuffed with cod). The huge *chuletón* (T-bone steak), seared over charcoal and sprinkled with sea salt, is for two or more; order *cogollo de lechuga* (lettuce hearts) to accompany. The *kokotxas de merluza* (hake jowls) are supremely light and aromatic. *Tirso de Molina 7 (upstairs at back), Lavapiés, tel. 91/369–1617; Pedro Muguruza 8, Chamartín, tel. 91/345–3696. Reservations essential. AE, DC, MC, V. No dinner Sun.*

$$–$$$$ **CASA BENIGNO.** A specialist in Mediterranean cuisine, this hideaway in northeastern Madrid is best known for its rice dishes, including *arroz a la banda* (rice with pre-shelled seafood) and the best paella in town. King Juan Carlos is a regular. Accompany the culinary inventions with your choice of olive oil from a truly encyclopedic selection. Owner-creator Don Norberto takes gracious care of international diners, suggesting wines from all over the Iberian Peninsula and guiding you through the casual, understated premises. *Benigno Soto 9, Chamartín, tel. 91/416–9357. Reservations essential. AE, DC, MC, V. Closed Aug., Holy Week, and 1 wk at Christmas. No dinner Sun.*

$$–$$$$ EL CENADOR DEL PRADO. The name means "The Prado Dining
★ Room," and the settings are a Baroque salon and a plant-filled
conservatory. The Cenador's innovative menu has French and
Asian touches, as well as exotic Spanish dishes that rarely appear
in restaurants. The house specialty is *patatas a la importancia*
(sliced potatoes fried in a sauce of garlic, parsley, and clams); other
possibilities include shellfish consommé with ginger ravioli, veal
and eggplant in béchamel, and venison with prunes. For dessert
try the *bartolillos* (custard-filled pastries). *C. del Prado 4, Retiro, tel.
91/429–1561. AE, DC, MC, V. Closed Sun. and 1 wk in Aug. No lunch Sat.*

$$–$$$$ EL PESCADOR. The traditional belief that seafood served in
★ Madrid is fresher than in coastal towns where it was caught seems
almost plausible here. Among the tapas, the *salpicón de mariscos*
(mussels, lobster, shrimp, and onions in vinaigrette) is nonpareil.
Lenguado Evaristo (grilled sole), named for the restaurant's owner,
is a standout. Boisterous and ebullient, with such rustic touches
as lobster-pot lamps, red-and-white-checked tablecloths, and
rough-hewn posts and beams, this is a seafood emporium to
take seriously. *José Ortega y Gasset 75, Salamanca, tel. 91/402–1290.
MC, V. Closed Sun. and Aug.*

$$–$$$$ LA TRAINERA. With its nautical theme and maze of little dining
rooms, this informal restaurant is all about fresh seafood—the
best money can buy. Crab, lobster, shrimp, mussels, and a dozen
other types of shellfish are served by weight in *raciones* (large
portions). Although many Spanish diners share several plates of
these shellfish as their entire meal, the grilled hake, sole, or
turbot makes an unbeatable second course. To accompany the
legendary *carabineros* (giant scarlet shrimp), skip the listless house
wine and go for a bottle of Albariño, from the southern Galician
coast. *Lagasca 60, Salamanca, tel. 91/576–8035. AE, MC, V. Closed Sun.
and Aug.*

$$–$$$$ PEDRO LARUMBE. This restaurant is literally the pinnacle of the
ABC shopping center between Paseo de la Castellana and Calle
Serrano. Dining quarters include a summer roof terrace, glassed

in for the winter, and an Andalusian patio. Chef-owner Pedro Larumbe is known for his presentations of such contemporary dishes as *cazuela de cocochas con patatas al pil-pil* (a casserole of tender cheeks of hake, cooked in their own juices combined with oil and garlic, and served with potatoes). There's a salad bar at lunchtime, and the dessert buffet is an art exhibit. A good wine list complements the fare. *Paseo de la Castellana 34, at C. Serrano 61, Salamanca, tel. 91/575–1112. AE, DC, MC, V. Closed Sun., 1 wk at Easter, and 2 wks in Aug. No lunch Sat.*

$–$$$$ LA GAMELLA. American-born chef Dick Stephens has created a
★ new, reasonably priced menu at this perennially popular dinner spot. The sophisticated rust-red dining room, batik tablecloths, oversize plates, and attentive service remain the same, but much of the nouvelle cuisine has been replaced by more traditional fare, such as chicken in garlic, beef bourguignonne, and steak tartare à la Jack Daniels. A few of the old signature dishes, like sausage-and-red-pepper quiche and bittersweet chocolate pâté, remain. The lunchtime menú del día is a great value. *Alfonso XII 4, Retiro, tel. 91/532–4509. AE, DC, MC, V. Closed Sun. and last 2 wks in Aug. No lunch Sat.*

$$–$$$ EL BORBOLLÓN. For nearly two decades the friendly Castro family has run this elegant yet comfortable restaurant and bar between Paseo de Recoletos and Calle Serrano, with pink tablecloths, fresh flowers, and paintings of country scenes. Chef Eduardo prepares French-Basque fare, including crepes, *carré* (a prime cutlet or chop) of lamb, fresh sea bass, turbot, and hake, plus rich game dishes in season. Alfonso Castro, the sommelier, offers good wines and brandies. Dinner reservations are wise; at lunchtime, there's food at the bar. *Paseo Recoletos 7, Centro, tel. 91/431–4134. AE, DC, MC, V. Closed Sun. and Aug.*

$–$$$ CASA CIRIACO. One of Madrid's most traditional restaurants, Ciriaco has hosted a long list of Spain's illustrious, from royalty to philosophers, painters, and bullfighters. With simple home cooking in an unpretentious environment, Casa Ciriaco will serve you a flagon of Valdepeñas or a split of a Rioja reserva to accompany the specialty of *perdiz con favas* (partridge with broad beans). The *judias con liebre* (white beans with hare) is another favorite. *C. Mayor 84, Centro, tel. 91/559–5066. AE, MC, V. Closed Wed. and Aug.*

$–$$$ **CASA LASTRA.** Established in 1926, this Asturian tavern is popular with Lavapiés locals. The rustic, half-tile walls strung with relics from the Asturian countryside include wooden clogs, cow bells, sausages and garlic. Specialties include *fabada* (Asturian white-beans stewed with sausage), *fabas con almejas* (white beans with clams), and *queso de cabrales*, mega-aromatic cheese made in the Picos de Europa from a mixture of milk from cows, goats, and sheep. Great hunks of crisp bread and hard Asturian cider complement a hearty meal; desserts include tangy baked apples. *Olivar 3, Lavapiés, tel. 91/369–0837. AE, MC, V. Closed Wed. and July. No dinner Sun.*

$–$$$ **CASA PACO.** This Castilian tavern wouldn't have looked out of place
★ two or three centuries ago. Squeeze past the old, zinc-top bar, crowded with Madrileños downing shots of Valdepeñas red wine, and into the tile dining rooms. Feast on thick slabs of red meat, sizzling on plates so hot that it continues to cook at your table. The Spanish consider overcooking a sin, so expect looks of dismay if you ask for your meat well done (*bien hecho*). You order by weight, so remember that a *medio kilo* is more than a pound. To start, try the *pisto manchego* (the La Mancha version of ratatouille) or the Castilian *sopa de ajo* (garlic soup). *Puerta Cerrada 11, Centro, tel. 91/ 366–3166. Reservations essential. AE, DC, MC, V. Closed Sun. and Aug.*

$–$$$ **CASA VALLEJO.** With its homey dining room, friendly staff, creative menu, and reasonable prices, Casa Vallejo is a well-kept secret of low-budget foodies. Try the tomato, zucchini, and cheese tart or artichokes and clams to start; follow up with duck in prune sauce or meatballs made with lamb, almonds, and pine nuts. The fudge-and-raspberry pie alone is worth the trip. *San Lorenzo 9, Centro, tel. 91/308–6158. Reservations essential. MC, V. Closed Aug. and Sun. No dinner Mon.*

$–$$$ IROCO. This large, stylish, green-wall establishment is popular with businesspeople at lunch hour and trendy folk in the evening. Try to dine on the garden patio, where Crown Prince Felipe has been spotted. The *nueva cocina* (nouvelle cuisine) is well presented, and the set lunch menu is good value. Classic dishes include prawn rolls, hake in green asparagus sauce, and chocolate mousse. *Velázquez 18, Salamanca, tel. 91/431–7381. Reservations essential. AE, DC, MC, V.*

$–$$$ JULIÁN DE TOLOSA. On the corner of Cava Baja and Almendro, this rustic yet designer-decorated spot is famous for *alubias pintas* (red kidney beans) from the Basque town of Tolosa. The *bellota* (acorn-fed) ham here is fine-sliced and unctuous, while the two-person *txuletón* (28-ounce beefsteak) is excellent. The *pimientos de piquillo* (roasted sweet red peppers) come to the table sizzling and may be the best in the world. Try a Basque *txakolí* (tart, young white wine) with your first course and a Ribera de Duero later. Let maître d' and owner Gotzone talk you into a diminutive flask of *patxarán*, the famous Basque sloe-berry liqueur, over coffee. Reservations are essential. *Cava Baja 18, Centro, tel. 91/365–8210. AE, DC, MC, V. Closed Sun.*

$–$$$ LA BOLA. ★ First opened as a *botellería* (wine shop) in 1802, La Bola developed slowly into a tapas bar and eventually into a full-fledged restaurant. Tradition is the main draw; blood-red paneling outside beckons you into the original bar and the cozy dining nooks, decorated with polished wood, Spanish tile, and lace curtains. The restaurant still belongs to the founding family, with the seventh generation currently in training. Dinner is served, but the house specialty is cocido a la madrileña, served only at lunch. *C. de la Bola 5, Ópera, tel. 91/547–6930. No credit cards. No dinner Sun.*

$–$$$ LA CAVA REAL. Wine connoisseurs love the intimate look and feel of this small bar-restaurant, which was Madrid's first true wine bar when it opened in 1983. Still part of Spain's largest wine club (warning: no beer!), it's also open to the public, smartly decorated in plush reds and dark browns. There are a staggering 350 wines

madrid dining

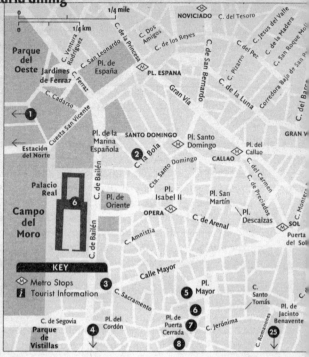

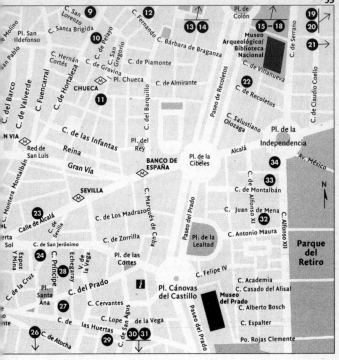

La Trucha, 28

La Vaca
Verónica, 30

Las Cuevas de
Luis Candelas, 5

Lhardy, 24

Nabucco, 10

Pedro
Larumbe, 16

Santceloni, 18

Taberna
Carmencita, 11

Viridiana, 32

Zalacaín, 15

on offer, including 50 by the glass. The charming and experienced maître d', Chema Gómez, can help you choose. Chef Javier Collar designs good-value menus around various wines, and the à la carte selection is plentiful, mainly *nueva cocina* with game in season as well as fancy desserts and cheeses. *Espronceda 34, Chamberí, tel. 91/ 442–5432. Reservations essential. AE, DC, MC, V. Closed Sun. and Aug.*

$–$$$ **LAS CUEVAS DE LUIS CANDELAS.** Hidden just off the southwest corner of the Plaza Mayor, this "cave" is said to be the oldest tavern in Madrid and feels like the medieval cellar of a Spanish mansion. You're greeted by a host dressed as the 19th-century bandit himself, and you enter through a long bar where noisy regulars drink and munch tapas. A low stone archway leads to a quieter area where you can sit on low benches, drink from a ceramic jar, and eat *raciones* of such tapas as mushrooms in garlic and cured ham. Farther inside the "cave" are the dining areas, with painted scenes of old Madrid. Huge and heavy portions of barbecued meats are the specialty. A strolling guitar player adds to the enchanting, if slightly touristy, atmosphere. *Cuchilleros 1, Centro, tel. 91/366–5428. AE, MC, V.*

$–$$ **BOTÍN.** The *Guinness Book of Records* calls this the world's oldest
★ restaurant (1725), and Hemingway called it the best. The latter claim may be a bit over the top, but the restaurant is excellent and extremely charming (and so successful that the owners opened a "branch" in Miami, Florida). There are four floors of tile, wood-beam dining rooms, and, if you're seated upstairs you'll pass ovens dating back centuries. Musical groups called *tunas* often drop in to meander among the hordes. Specialties are *cochinillo asado* (roast suckling pig) and *cordero asado* (roast lamb), but you might also try the *estofada de perdiz* (stewed partridge). It is said that Goya washed dishes here before he made it as a painter. *Cuchilleros 17, off Plaza Mayor, Centro, tel. 91/366–4217. AE, DC, MC, V.*

$–$$ **CASA MINGO.** Resembling an Asturian cider tavern, Casa Mingo
★ is built into a stone wall beneath the Estación del Norte, across the street from the hermitage of San Antonio de la Florida. It's a

bustling place; you share long plank tables with other diners, and the only items on the menu are succulent roast chicken, salad, and sausages, all to be taken with *sidra* (hard cider). Small tables are set up on the sidewalk in summer. If you don't come early (1 for lunch, 8:30 for dinner), you may have to wait for a table. *Paseo de la Florida 2, Moncloa, tel. 91/547–7918. Reservations not accepted. No credit cards.*

$–$$ LA BIOTIKA. A vegetarian's dream in the heart of the bar district just east of Plaza Santa Ana, this small, cozy restaurant serves macrobiotic vegetarian food seven days a week. Enormous salads, hearty soups, fresh bread, and creative tofu dishes make the meal flavorful as well as healthy. A small shop at the entrance sells macrobiotic groceries. *Amor de Dios 3, Santa Ana, tel. 91/429–0780. No credit cards.*

$–$$ LA CACHARRERÍA. The name of this restaurant means "junkyard," and it's reflected in the decor—a mix of dusty calico, old lace, and gilt mirrors, all tucked into the medieval quarter. The cooking, however, is upscale, with a market-based menu that changes daily and an excellent selection of wines. Venison stew and tuna steaks with *cava* (sparkling white wine from Catalonia) and leeks have been among the specialties. Save room for the homemade lemon tart. *Morería 9, Centro, tel. 91/365–3930. AE, DC, MC, V. Closed Sun.*

$–$$ LA TRUCHA. This Andalusian deep-fry specialist is one of the
★ happiest places in Madrid. The staff is jovial, and the house specialty, *trucha la truchana* (crisped trout stuffed with ample garlic and diced *jabugo* ham) is a work of art. Other star entrées are *chopitos* (baby squid), *pollo al ajillo* (chunks of chicken in crisped garlic), and *espárragos trigueros* (wild asparagus). Jarras (pitchers) of chilled Valdepeñas, a young Beaujolais-like claret, seem to function as laughing gas in this magic little bistro. The Nuñez de Arce branch, just down from the Hotel Reina Victoria, is usually less crowded. *Manuel Fernandez y Gonzalez 3, Santa Ana; Nuñez de Arce 6, Santa Ana, tel. 91/429–3778. AE, MC, V. Closed Sun. Nuñez de Arce branch also closed Aug.*

$–$$ LA VACA VERÓNICA. In the golden-age literary quarter, this romantic little hideaway is gathering a following for its *carne a la brasa* (meat cooked over coals), *pescado a la sal* (fish cooked in a shell of salt), homemade pastas with various seafood dressings, and terrific salads. The *pasta a los carabineros* (pasta with scarlet shrimp) is said to be seducing everyone from Penelope Cruz to Alie Nicholas. *Moratín 38, Santa Ana, tel. 91/429–7827. AE, DC, MC, V.*

$–$$ NABUCCO. With pastel-washed walls and subtle lighting from gigantic wrought-iron candelabras, this pizzeria and trattoria is a trendy but elegant haven in gritty Chueca. Fresh bread sticks and garlic olive oil show up within minutes of your arrival. The spinach, ricotta, and walnut ravioli is heavenly, and the pizza is also tasty. Considering the ambience and quality, the bill is a pleasant surprise. *Hortaleza 108, Chueca, tel. 91/310–0611. AE, MC, V.*

$–$$ TABERNA CARMENCITA. Just two minutes' north of the Gran Vía–Calle Alcalá intersection is an old Madrid favorite for lunches and light dinners. Now part of priest-restaurateur Patxo de Lezama's sprawling gastronomic empire (which extends to Washington, D.C.), this ceramic-tile tavern retains much of the atmosphere it had in the mid-20th century, when Carmencita herself cared for customers as though they were long-lost children. Try the *chipirones en su tinta* (squid in its ink) and *sopa de pescado* (fish soup). *Libertad 16, Centro, tel. 91/531–6612. AE, DC, MC, V. Closed Sun. No lunch Sat.*

$ CHAMPAGNERÍA GALA. Hidden on a back street not far from Calle Atocha and the Reina Sofía museum, this cheerful Mediterranean restaurant is usually packed thanks to its fixed-price three-course menus with wine, which offer a choice of paellas, *fideuas* (paellas with noodles instead of rice), risottos, and hearty bean stews. Only *cava*, Catalan sparkling wine, costs extra. The front dining area is a kaleidoscope of painted color, particularly red; the back area incorporates trees and plants in a glassed-in patio. *Moratín 22, Santa Ana, tel. 91/429–2562. Reservations essential. No credit cards.*

$ CIAO. Always noisy and packed, Ciao is Madrid's best Italian restaurant. Homemade pastas, like tagliatelle with wild mushrooms and *panzarotti* stuffed with spinach and ricotta, are popular as inexpensive main courses; but the kitchen also turns out credible osso buco and veal scallopini, accompanied by a good selection of Italian wines. Mirrored walls and sleek black furniture convincingly evoke fashionable Milan. A second location (Apodaca 20, Chamberí, tel. 91/447–0036), run by the owner's sons and daughter, also serves pizza. *Argensola 7, Centro, tel. 91/308–2519. Reservations essential. AE, DC, MC, V. Closed Sept. and Sun. No lunch Sat.*

In This Chapter

Updated by George Semler

shopping

MADRID HAS FAR MORE ON OFFER THAN LLADRÓ porcelain and
bullfighting posters—Spain has become one of the world's centers
for design of every kind. You'll have no trouble finding traditional
crafts, such as ceramics, guitars, and leather goods (albeit not at
countryside prices), but at this point the city is more like Rodeo
Drive than the bargain bin. Known for contemporary furniture
and decorative items as well as chic clothing, shoes, and jewelry,
Spain's capital has become stiff competition for Barcelona. Most
shops accept most major credit cards.

DEPARTMENT STORES

EL CORTE INGLÉS. Spain's largest department store carries the
best selection of everything, from auto parts to groceries to
designer fashions. *Preciados 3, Sol, tel. 91/531–9619; 901/122122
general information; 902/400222 ticket sales; Goya 76 and 87,
Salamanca, tel. 91/432–9300; Princesa 56, Centro, tel. 91/454–6000;
Serrano 47, Salamanca, tel. 91/432–5490; Raimundo Fernández
Villaverde 79, Chamartín, tel. 91/418–8800.*

ZARA. For those with young tastes and slim pocketbooks
(picture hip clothes that you'll throw away in about six months),
Zara has the latest looks for men, women, and children. *Centro
Comercial ABC, Serrano 61, Salamanca, tel. 91/575–6334; Gran Vía 32,
Centro, tel. 91/522–9727; Princesa 63, Centro, tel. 91/543–2415;
Conde de Peñalver 4, Salamanca, tel. 91/435–4135.*

SHOPPING DISTRICTS

Madrid has two main shopping areas. The first, around the Puerta del Sol, includes the major department stores (El Corte Inglés, the French music-and-book chain FNAC, etc.) and mid-range shops in the streets nearby. The second area, far more elegant and expensive, is in the northwestern Salamanca district, bounded roughly by Serrano, Goya, and Conde de Peñalver. These streets, just off the Plaza de Colón (particularly Calle Serrano), have the widest selection of smart boutiques and designer fashions—think Prada, Armani, and Donna Karan New York, as well as renowned Spanish designers such as Sybilla and Josep Font-Luz Diaz.

GALERÍAS DEL PRADO (Plaza de las Cortés 7, Centro) is an attractive mall tucked under the Westin Palace on the Paseo del Prado. Shop here for fine books and foods, clothing, leather, and art. Madrid's newest mall is a four-decker: the **CENTRO COMERCIAL ABC** (Paseo de la Castellana 34, at Serrano 61, Salamanca), named for the daily newspaper founded on the premises in the 19th century. The building has an ornate tile facade; inside, a large café is surrounded by shops, including leather stores and hairdressers. The fourth-floor restaurant has a rooftop terrace. For street-chic shopping closer to medieval Madrid, check out the playful window displays at the **MADRID FUSION CENTRO DE MODA** (Plaza Tirso de Molina 15, Lavapiés, tel. 91/369–0018), where Spanish design houses fill five floors with faux furs, funky jewelry, and Madrid's most eccentric collection of shoes.

FLEA MARKET

On Sunday morning, Calle de Ribera de Curtidores is closed to traffic and jammed with outdoor booths selling everything under the sun—its weekly transformation into **EL RASTRO**. The crowds grow so thick that it takes a while just to advance a few feet amid the hawkers and gawkers. Pickpockets abound here.

Hang on to your purse and wallet, and be especially careful if you choose to bring a camera. The flea market sprawls into most of the surrounding streets, with certain areas specializing in particular products. Many of the goods are wildly overpriced. But what goods! The Rastro has everything from antique furniture to exotic parrots and cuddly puppies; from pirated cassette tapes of flamenco music to key chains emblazoned with symbols of the CNT, Spain's old anarchist trade union. Practice your Spanish by bargaining with the vendors over paintings, colorful Gypsy oxen yokes, heraldic iron gates, new and used clothes, and even hashish pipes. They may not lower their prices, but sometimes they'll throw in a handmade bracelet or a stack of postcards to sweeten the deal.

Plaza General Vara del Rey has some of the Rastro's best antiques, and the streets beyond—Calles Mira el Río Alta and Mira el Río Baja—have some truly magnificent junk and bric-a-brac. The market shuts down shortly after 2 PM, in time for a street party to start in the area known as La Latina, centered on the bar El Viajero in Plaza Humilladero.

Off the Ribera are two *galerías*, courtyards with higher-quality, higher-priced antiques shops. Near the top of the Rastro, stop into **Bar Santurce** (C. Amazonas 14, Lavapiés) for sardines, Galician *pimientos de Padrón* (red peppers, some hot), and calamari.

SPECIALTY STORES

Books

CASA DEL LIBRO (Maestro Victoria 3, Centro, tel. 91/521–4898), not far from the Puerta del Sol, has an impressive collection of English-language books, including city guides and translated Spanish classics. It's also a good source for maps, cookbooks, and gifts. **BOOKSELLERS** (José Abascal 48, Chamberí, tel. 91/442–8104), just off the upper Castellana near the Hotel Miguel

Angel, has a large selection of books in English. For travel books, including books about Madrid in English, seek out **TIERRA DE FUEGO** (C. del Pez 21, Centro, tel. 91/521–3962) in the Barrio de Maravillas, two blocks north of the central Gran Vía. Established in 1950, **LA TIENDA VERDE** (Maudes 23 and 38, Chamberí, tel. 91/535–3810) is perfect for outdoor enthusiasts planning hikes, mountain-climbing expeditions, spelunking trips, and so forth, with detailed maps and Spanish-language guidebooks.

Boutiques and Fashion

ADOLFO DOMÍNGUEZ (Serrano 96, Salamanca, tel. 91/576–7053; and six other locations) is one of Spain's best-known designers, with lines for both men and women. Prominent young designer **JESÚS DEL POZO** (Almirante 9, Salamanca, tel. 91/531–3646) also caters to both sexes; his boutique is an excellent, if pricey, place to try on some classic Spanish style. Since the turn of the 20th century **SESEÑA** (De la Cruz 23, Sol, tel. 91/531–6840) has outfitted international celebrities in wool and velvet capes, some lined with red satin. **SYBILLA** (Jorge Juan 12, Salamanca, tel. 91/578–1322) is the studio of Spain's best-known female designer, whose fluid dresses and hand-knit sweaters have made her a favorite with Danish supermodel Helena Christensen.

Ceramics

ANTIGUA CASA TALAVERA (Isabel la Católica 2, Centro, tel. 91/547–3417) is the best of Madrid's many ceramics shops. Despite the name, the finest ware sold here is from Manises, near Valencia, but the blue-and-yellow Talavera ceramics are also excellent. **CÁNTARO** (Flor Baja 8, Centro, tel. 91/547–9514) sells handmade ceramics. **CERÁMICA EL ALFAR** (Claudio Coello 112, Salamanca, tel. 91/411–3587) is laden with pottery from around Spain. **SAGARDELOS** (Zurbano 46, Chamberí, tel. 91/310–4830), specializing in modern Spanish ceramics from Galicia, has breakfast sets, coffee pots, and objets d'art.

Crafts and Design

CASA JULIA (Almirante 1, Centro, tel. 91/522–0270) is an artistic showcase, with two floors of tasteful antiques, paintings by up-and-coming artists, and furniture in experimental designs. It's a great place to hunt for nontraditional souvenirs. **EL ARCO** (Plaza Mayor 9, Centro, tel. 91/365–2680) has contemporary handicrafts from all over Spain, including modern ceramics, handblown glassware, jewelry, and leather items as well as a whimsical collection of pendulum clocks.

Fans

CASA DE DIEGO (Puerta del Sol 12, Sol, tel. 91/522–6643), established in 1853, stocks fans, umbrellas, and classic Spanish walking sticks with ornamented silver handles. The British royal family buys autograph fans here—white kidskin fans for signing on special occasions.

Food and Wine

The Club Gourmet sections in stores sell Spanish wines, olive oils, and food. Handily near Plaza Santa Ana and Plaza de las Cortés, **GONZÁLEZ** (C. Léon 21, Santa Ana, tel. 91/429–5618) has fine Spanish wines, olive oils, cheeses, hams, dried *pulses* (seeds in a pod), and other foods. Try the wine bar in back. **LAVININA** (José Ortega y Gasset 16, Salamanca, tel. 91/426–0604) claims to be the largest wine store in Europe and has a large selection of bottles, books, and bar accessories. The upscale chain **MALLORCA** (Velázquez 59, Salamanca, tel. 91/431–9909; Serrano 6, Salamanca, tel. 91/577–1859; Centro Comercial, Goya 6, Salamanca, tel. 91/577–2123) sells prepared meals, cocktail canapés, chocolates, and wines and has tapas counters. Just across from eateries Los Gabrieles and La Trucha, behind Plaza Santa Ana, **MARIANO AGUADO** (C. Echegaray 19, Santa Ana, tel. 91/429–6088) is a charming 150-year-old wine store with a quaint ceiling mural and a wide selection of fine wines and spirits.

Hats

Founded in 1894, **CASA YUSTAS** (Plaza Mayor 30, Sol, tel. 91/366–5084) has headgear ranging from the old three-corner, patent-leather hats of the Guardia Civil to fashionable ladies' hats to Basque berets to black Andalusian *sombreros de mayoral*. Designed as hands-free umbrellas for the rainy Cantabrian coast, Basque berets are much wider than those worn by the French and make excellent gifts.

Kitchenware

A pleasing mixture of tradition and high style, **ALAMBIQUE** (C. de la Bola, Opera, tel. 91/547–8827), on Plaza de la Encarnación, has everything from earthenware and Asturian cider glasses to cookbooks and a cooking school.

Leather Goods

On a street full of bargain shoe stores (*muestrarios*), **CALIGAE** (Augusto Figueroa 27, Salamanca, tel. 91/531–5343) is probably the best of the bunch. Posh **LOEWE** (Serrano 26 and 34, Salamanca, tel. 91/577–6056; Gran Vía 8, Centro, tel. 91/532–7024; Westin Palace, Centro, tel. 91/429–8530) has ultra–high-quality designer purses, accessories, and clothing made of buttery-soft leather in dyed, jewel-like colors. Prices can hit the stratosphere. **TENORIO** (Plaza de la Provincia 6, Centro, tel. 91/366–4440) is where you'll find those fine old boots of Spanish leather, made to order with workmanship that should last a lifetime and is priced accordingly, starting at €660.

Music

JOSÉ RAMIREZ (C. La Paz 8, Centro, tel. 91/531–4229) has provided Spain and the rest of the world with guitars since 1882, and his store includes a museum of antique instruments. Prices for new ones start at €90, though the top concert models are closer to €6,000. **REAL MÚSICA** (Carlos III 1, Centro, tel. 91/541–3007), around the corner from the Teatro Real, is a music lover's dream, with books, CDs, sheet music, memorabilia, guitars, and a knowledgeable staff.

In This Chapter

Updated by George Semler

outdoor activities and sports

MADRILEÑOS ARE A VIGOROUS, joyful lot, famous for their ability to defy sleep. They embrace their city's vibrant sports activities with as much zest as they do its cultural opportunities and nightlife. And you need only witness a bullfight at Las Ventas or a Real Madrid soccer match at Santiago Bernabeu Stadium to see that, in some cases, culture and sport are one in the same. What's more, Spain's fair weather is ideally suited to spending time outdoors virtually year-round. In summer, however, it's best to restrict physical activity to early morning or late afternoon.

PARTICIPANT SPORTS

Golf

Eleven golf courses surround Madrid and more are on the way. The successes of Seve Ballesteros, José María Olazabal, and Sergio García have created a new surge of golf interest in Spain. Proof of membership in a home golf club is usually all you need to qualify to pay the approximately €40–€50 (weekdays) greens fees. Prices double on weekends and holidays. Playing golf at La Herrería Club's 18-hole course in the shadow of the monolithic Monastery of San Lorenzo del Escorial is one of Spain's great golfing experiences. **GOLF OLIVAR DE LA HINOJOSA** (Av. Dublín s/n, Barajas, tel. 91/721–1889), in Campo de las Naciones outside town, is open to the public with two courses (one 18 holes, one 9) and golf lessons. **LA HERRERÍA CLUB** (Ctra. Robledo de Chavela s/n, Escorial, tel. 91/890–1889), in San Lorenzo de Escorial, is open to the public. **LA MORALEJA CLUB** (Paseo Marquesa Viuda de Aldama 50, La Moraleja, tel. 91/650–0700), just north of Madrid, has a pair of 18-hole courses open to nonmembers.

Jogging

Your best bet for jogging is the Parque del Retiro, where a path circles the park and others weave under trees and through formal gardens. The Casa de Campo is crisscrossed by numerous, sunnier trails.

Swimming

Madrid has an antidote to the dry, sometimes intense heat of the summer months—a superb system of clean, popular, well-run municipal swimming pools (admission about €2). The biggest and best—fitted with a comfortable, tree-shaded restaurant—is in the **CASA DE CAMPO** (take the metro to Lago and walk up the hill a few yards, Moncloa; tel. 91/463–0050). In the city center, the **PISCINA CANAL ISABEL II** (Plaza Juan Zorrila, entrance off Av. de Filipinas, Chamartín, no phone) has diving boards and a wading pool for kids.

Tennis

CLUB DE TENIS CHAMARTÍN (Federico Salmon 2, Chamartín, tel. 91/345–2500) has 28 courts and is open to the public. There are public courts in the **CASA DE CAMPO** (Moncloa; tel. 91/463–0050) and on the Avenida de Vírgen del Puerto, behind the Palacio Real.

SPECTATOR SPORTS

Soccer

Spain's number-one sport is known locally as *fútbol*. Madrid has three major teams, Real Madrid, Atlético Madrid, and Rayo Vallecano. For tickets, either call a week in advance to reserve and pick them up at the stadium or stand in line at the stadium of your choice. The **ESTADIO SANTIAGO BERNABEU** (Paseo de la Castellana 140, Chamartín, tel. 91/398–4300), which seats 75,000, is home to Real Madrid, winner of a staggering eight European Champion's Cups over the last 50 years. Atlético Madrid plays at the **ESTADIO VICENTE CALDERÓN** (Virgen del Puerto 67, Arganzuela, tel. 91/366–4707 or 91/364–0888), on the edge of the Manzanares river south of town. Rayo Vallecano plays at **ESTADIO DEL RAYO** (Arroyo del Olivar 49, Vallecas, tel. 91/478–2253).

In This Chapter

Updated by George Semler

nightlife and the arts

NIGHTLIFE—OR LA MARCHA—reaches legendary heights in Madrid. It has been said that Madrileños rarely sleep, largely because they spend so much time in bars—not drunk, but socializing in the easy, sophisticated way that's unique to this city. This is true of old as well as young, and it's not uncommon for children to play on the sidewalks past midnight while multigenerational families and friends convene over coffee or cocktails at an outdoor café. The streets best known for their social scenes, however, do attract a younger clientele; these include Huertas, Moratín, Segovia, Victoria, and the areas around the Plaza Santa Ana and the Plaza de Anton Martín. The adventurous may want to explore the scruffier bar district around the Plaza Dos de Mayo, in the Malasaña area, where trendy, smoke-filled hangouts line both sides of Calle San Vicente Ferrer. A few blocks east are the haunts of Chueca, where tattoo studios and street-chic boutiques break up the endless alleys of gay and lesbian bars, techno discos, and after-hours clubs.

As Madrid's reputation as a vibrant, contemporary arts center has grown, artists and performers have arrived in droves. Consult the weekly *Guía del Ocio* (published Monday) or daily listings in the leading newspaper, *El País*, both of which are understandable even if you don't read much Spanish.

BARS AND TAVERNS

The practice of spending the evening wandering from bar to bar and eating tapas is so popular that the Spanish have a verb to describe it: *tapear*. Madrid's selection is endless; the best-known tapas bars are the *cuevas* clustered around Cava de San Miguel.

Bars

ALHAMBRA. This one-room tavern has been serving excellent wine, beer, and tapas to a gregarious crowd since 1929. Alhambra opens at an eye-popping 9:30 AM; around midnight it fills up, the windows get steamy, and the crowd does pseudo-*sevillana* dance moves to traditional music. When it's packed, they jump right onto the wooden tabletops without missing a beat. *Victoria 9, Sol, tel. 91/521–0708.*

CAFE GIJÓN. Madrid's most famous literary café has hosted highbrow *tertulias*, discussion groups that meet regularly to hash out the political and artistic issues of the day, since the 19th century. *Paseo de Recoletos 21, Chamberí, tel. 91/521–5425.*

EL CLANDESTINO. Run by a French couple who seem to be Spaniards at heart, this bar-café is a hidden, low-key hot spot with a local following: atmosphere without attitude. Impromptu jam sessions are rounded out by two floors alternating mellow jazz with house and ambient music. *Barquillo 34, Centro, tel. 91/521–5563.*

HARD ROCK CAFE. Wildly popular with young Spaniards, Madrid's version of the U.S. classic opened in 1994, serving up the usual drinks, burgers, and salads with a heavy dose of loud music. *Paseo de la Castellana 2, Centro, tel. 91/436–4340.*

LOS GABRIELES. This building is included in most Madrid tourist literature for its remarkable tiled walls—advertisements from the turn of the 20th century, when this was a high-class brothel. Drinks are unusually pricey. *Echegaray 17, Santa Ana, tel. 91/429–6261.*

OLIVER. Here are two bars in one: afternoons and evenings, an upstairs lounge and restaurant; late at night, a full-fledged

Chueca disco in the brick-lined basement cavern. *Almirante 12, Centro, tel. 91/521–7379.*

PALACIO DE GAVIRIA. Hidden away on a tawdry commercial street between Puerta del Sol and the Royal Palace, this restored 19th-century palace was allegedly built to house one of Queen Isabel II's lovers. An exotic maze, it now offers drinks, with a disco and frequent late-night jazz in the mirrored ballroom. *Arenal 9, Sol, tel. 91/526–6069.*

SOHO. Something of a slice of New York in the Salamanca district, Soho has an eclectic menu that includes exotic island drinks as well as Spanish variants of Tex-Mex cuisine. It's filled with rap and reggae fans. *Jorge Juan 50, Salamanca, tel. 91/577–8973. Closed Sun.*

TABERNA DE ANTONIO SANCHEZ. Thought to be the oldest tavern in Madrid, this historic spot was traced by the late critic and *literato* Antonio Diaz-Cañabate to the late 18th century. Order wine and tapas at the old zinc bar in front; head to the back for a full meal. *Mesón de Paredes 13, Lavapiés, tel. 91/539–7826.*

VIVA MADRID. This popular bar has a Brassai motif and a serious personality. Packed with Spaniards and foreigners, it has become something of a singles scene. There are tables and bar food in the rear. *Manuel Fernández y González 7, Santa Ana, tel. 91/429–3640.*

Tapas Bars

BOCAÍTO. This cozy spot with three doors on Calle Libertad has twin bars and a restaurant serving no fewer than 130 specialties, all lovingly prepared. The *pescaito* (deep-fried whitebait) is the best in Madrid. *Libertad 6, Centro, tel. 91/532–1219.*

★ **EL ABUELO.** A favorite even in the tapa-saturated Plaza Santa Ana area, El Abuelo (The Grandfather) serves only two tapas, and does them better than anyone: grilled shrimp and shrimp sautéed with garlic. House tradition is to drink the sweet, red homemade house wine while tossing shrimp shells onto the floor. *Victoria 12, Sol, tel. 91/521–2319.*

EL REY DE PIMIENTO. This bar serves some 40 different kinds of tapas, including, in keeping with its name (The Pepper King), roasted red pimientos as well as the intermittently hot pimientos *de padrón. Plaza Puerta Cerrada 4, Plaza Mayor, tel. 91/365–2473.*

EL VENTORRILLO. Try to come here between May and October, when tables are set up in the shady park of Las Vistillas overlooking the city's western edge. Specialties include croquettes and mushrooms. This is Madrid's best place to watch the sun go down. *C. Bailén 14, Centro, tel. 91/366–3578.*

GONZÁLEZ. Founded in 1931, González is run by Vicente Carmona, once a professor of Spanish literature in the United States. The smart, trendy deli in front sells (and will ship) Spanish wines, olive oils, liqueurs, hams, cheeses, cold cuts, and pastries. The paneled wine bar in back is a great place to sample the wares. *C. Léon 12, Santa Ana, tel. 91/429–5618.*

★ **LA CHATA.** Locals frequent this stylized *castizo* tapas bar, its walls and tree-trunk beams festooned with hams, sausages, chili peppers, and bullfight photos. You get an excellent free tapa with a drink; then choose from the selection of snacks on display or some great *revuelto con ajetes* (scrambled eggs with green garlic tops). A slate shows wines available by the glass. *Cava Baja 24, Plaza Mayor, tel. 91/366–1458.*

LA DOLORES. Crowded and noisy, this bar serves the best draft beer in Madrid. Located just behind the Westin Palace, it has very few tables in back. *Plaza de Jesús 4, Santa Ana, tel. 91/429–2243.*

★ **LA TRUCHA.** Savor the exquisite tapas and such touches as hanging hams and garlic. House favorites are the enormous *plato de pescaditos fritos*, an assortment of fried fish, and *plato de ahumados*, a sampling of smoked-fish delicacies on toast. A terrace invites alfresco nibbling in summer. *Manuel Fernández y González 3, Santa Ana, tel. 91/429–5833.*

MESÓN GALLEGO. This hole-in-the-wall serves wonderfully hearty Galician potato soup (a famous cure for those who've drunk too much) called *caldo gallego*. Not for everyone is the Ribeiro, the somewhat acidic white wine made with grapes from Galician riverbanks. *León 4, Santa Ana, tel. 91/429–8997.*

MUSEO DEL JAMÓN. A small Madrid chain, the Ham Museum has become an institution. The best tapas are, of course, the air-cured hams, which come from all over the country. Don't be daunted by the variety; go for ordinary *serrano* or, if you feel like a splurge, the delicious, acorn-fed *ibérico de bellota. Carrera de San Jerónimo 6, Sol, tel. 91/458–0163; Mayor 7, Sol, tel. 91/531–4550; Paseo del Prado 44, Retiro, tel. 91/420–2414.*

TABERNA DE CIEN VINOS. Popular with wine buffs on Madrid's tapas circuit, this wine bar is tucked into a charming old house with wooden shutters and stone columns. You can order a wide selection of Spanish wines by the glass, and the *raciones* are superb. *Nuncio 17, Lavapiés, tel. 91/365–4704.*

NIGHTLIFE

Cabaret

BERLIN CABARET (Costanilla de San Pedro 11, Centro, tel. 91/366–2034) professes to provide cabaret as it was performed in Berlin in the '30s. Combining magic, chorus girls, and ribaldry, it draws an eccentric crowd for vintage café theater. On weekends, the fun lasts until daybreak.

Discos

Madrid's oldest and hippest disco for wild, all-night dancing to an international music mix is **EL SOL** (C. Jardines 3, Centro, tel.

91/532–6490), open 'til 5:30 AM. There's live music around midnight Thursday, Friday, and Saturday. **AVE NOX** (Lagasca 31, Salamanca, tel. 91/576–9715) is a torrid music bar–disco in a converted chapel: vaulted ceiling, choir loft, and all. **JOY ESLAVA** (C. Arenal 11, Sol, tel. 91/366–3733), a downtown disco in a converted theater, is an old standby. **PACHÁ** (Barceló 11, Centro, tel. 91/447–0128) is always energetic. **FORTUNY** (Fortuny 34, Chamberí, tel. 91/319–0588) attracts a celebrity crowd, especially in summer, when the lush outdoor patio opens for partying under the stars. Put on your best dancing shoes: the door is ultraselective. Salsa has become a fixture in Madrid; check out the most spectacular moves at **AZÚCAR** (Paseo Reina Cristina 7, Atocha, tel. 91/501–6107). **CLAMORES** (Albuquerque 14, Chamberí, tel. 91/445–7938) offers live music and wildness until dawn. **GOLDEN GRAN VÍA** (Gran Vía 54, Centro, tel. 91/547–1130) is a hip spot with live performances on Sunday. **GOLDEN BOITE** (Duque de Sesto 54, Retiro, tel. 91/573–8775) is always hot from midnight to whenever things wear out. **CHANGÓ** (Covarrubias 42, Chamberí, tel. 91/446–0036) is a mega-disco with mind-numbingly constructed performers go-going on stage and general frenzy until first light and after. **HONKY TONK** (Covarrubias 42, Chamberí, tel. 91/445–6886) is a music bar with live performances open daily from nine to five (no, not that nine-to-five).

Nightclubs

Jazz, rock, flamenco, and classical music are all popular in Madrid's many small clubs.

AMADIS. Here, telephones on every table encourage people to call each other with invitations to dance. *Covarrubias 42 (underneath Luchana Cinema), Chamberí, tel. 91/446–0036.*

CAFÉ CENTRAL. Madrid's best-known jazz venue is chic, and the musicians are often internationally known. Performances are usually from 10 PM to midnight. *Plaza de Ángel 10, Santa Ana, tel. 91/369–4143.*

CAFE DEL FORO. This funky, friendly club on the edge of Malasaña has live music every night starting at 11:30 PM. *San Andrés 38, Santa Ana, tel. 91/445–3752.*

CAFÉ JAZZ POPULART. Blues, jazz, Brazilian music, reggae, and salsa start at 11 PM. *Huertas 22, Santa Ana, tel. 91/429–8407.*

CHOCOLATERÍA SAN GINÉS. Open from 6 PM to 7 AM, this is traditionally the last stop of the bleary-eyed after a night out. Stumble in for cups of thick *chocolate*, crisp *churros*, and a glass of water. *Pasadizo de San Ginés (enter by Arenal 11), Sol, tel. 91/365–6546. Closed Mon.*

CLAMORES. This famous jazz club serves a wide selection of French and Spanish champagnes. *Albuquerque 14, Chamberí, tel. 91/445–7938.*

NEGRA TOMASA. Under palm fronds and fishnets, the crowd drinks mojitos (sugar, crushed limes, mint, crushed ice, and flavored rum) to horns, maracas, and drums at this Cuban music bar. The house trio draws an international crowd on weekends. *C. Espoz y Mina and C. Cadiz, Santa Ana, tel. 91/523–5830.*

SIROCO. The music's live until 12:30 AM Thursday to Saturday; funk and techno reign until 6 AM. *San Dimas 3, Centro, tel. 91/593–3070.*

SURISTAN. Just off the Plaza Santa Ana, this is a café by day, a college bar by evening, and an avant-garde theater of sorts late at night. It's a hip indie spot for nightly rock and pop concerts, as well as occasional theater and readings. *La Cruz 7, Santa Ana, tel. 91/532–3909.*

TORERO. A thoroughly modern club despite its name, Torero is for the beautiful people—quite literally: a bouncer allows only those judged to be *gente guapa* (beautiful people) to enter. It's one of Madrid's most glamorous spots. *Cruz 26, Santa Ana, tel. 91/ 523–1129.*

THE ARTS

Seats for the classical performing arts are best purchased through your hotel concierge or at the hall itself. **EL CORTE INGLÉS** sells tickets for major pop concerts (tel. 902/400222). **FNAC** (Preciados 28, Sol, tel. 91/595–6100) sells tickets to musical events. **TELE-ENTRADAS** (tel. 902/101212) is a central ticket broker.

The Festival de Otoño (Autumn Festival), from late September to late November, blankets the city with pop concerts, poetry readings, flamenco, and ballet and theater from world-renowned companies. Other annual events include world-class bonanzas of film, contemporary art, and jazz, salsa, rock, and African music, all at very reasonable prices.

Concerts/Ballet

Convento de la Encarnación and the Real Academia de Bellas Artes de San Fernando host concerts, along with other venues.

The modern **AUDITORIO NACIONAL DE MÚSICA** (Príncipe de Vergara 146, Salamanca, tel. 91/337–0100, www. auditorionacional.mcu.es) is Madrid's main concert hall, with spaces for both symphonic and chamber music. The resplendent **TEATRO REAL** (Plaza de Isabel II, Opera, tel. 91/ 516–0660) hosts opera and ballet.

The subterranean **CENTRO CULTURAL DE LA VILLA** (Plaza de Colón, Salamanca, tel. 91/575–6080 information; 91/516–0606 tickets) has an eclectic program ranging from gospel and blues to flamenco and Celtic dance. The **FUNDACIÓN JUAN MARCH** (Castello 77, Salamanca, tel. 91/435–4240) offers chamber music Monday at noon, Wednesday at 7:30, and Saturday at noon.

Film

Of Madrid's 65 movie theaters, only nine show foreign films, generally in English, with original sound tracks and Spanish subtitles. These are listed in newspapers and in the *Guía de Ocio* under "v. o."—*versión original*, i.e., undubbed. Your best bet for catching a new release is the **IDEAL YELMO CINEPLEX** (Doctor Cortezo 6, Centro, tel. 91/369–2518). The excellent, classic v. o. films at the **FILMOTECA CINE DORÉ** (Santa Isabel 3, Lavapiés, tel. 91/369–1125) change daily. **ALPHAVILLE** (Martín de los Heros 14, Centro, tel. 91/584–4524) is a leading v. o. theater right off Plaza de España. **RENOIR PLAZA DE ESPAÑA** (Martín de los Heros 12, Centro, tel. 91/541–4100) offers v. o. films. **RENOIR RETIRO** (Narvaez 42, Retiro, tel. 91/541–4100) is a good movie-house break in the Retiro neighborhood. You'll find v. o. selections at **RENOIR CUATRO CAMINOS** (Raimundo Fernandez Villaverde 10, Chamberí, tel. 91/541–4100). **PRINCESA** (Princesa 3, Centro, tel. 91/541–4100) is a good option for original-version films.

Flamenco

Spain's best flamenco habitat is Andalusia, but if you won't be traveling south, here are a few possibilities. Note that prices for dinner and a show tend to be very high; you can save money by dining elsewhere and arriving in time for the show. Drinks are usually extra.

CAFÉ DE CHINITAS. It's expensive, but the flamenco here is the best in Madrid. Reserve in advance; shows often sell out. Performances are at 10:30 PM Monday–Saturday. *Torrija 7, Opera, tel. 91/559–5135.*

CASA PATAS. Along with tapas, this well-known space offers good, relatively pure (according to the performers) flamenco. Prices are more reasonable than elsewhere. Shows are at 10:30 PM Monday–Thursday, at midnight Friday–Sunday. *Canizares 10, Lavapiés, tel. 91/369–0496.*

Not a Night Owl?

You can learn a lot about a place if you take its pulse after dark. So even if you're the original early-to-bed type, there's every reason to vary your routine when you're away from home.

EXPERIENCE THE FAMILIAR IN A NEW PLACE Whether your thing is going to the movies or going to concerts, it's always different away from home. In clubs, new faces and new sounds add up to a different scene. Or you may catch movies you'd never see at home.

TRY SOMETHING NEW Do something you've never done before. It's another way to dip into the local scene. A simple suggestion: Go out later than usual—go dancing late and finish up with breakfast at dawn.

DO SOMETHING OFFBEAT Look into lectures and readings as well as author appearances in book stores. You may even meet your favorite novelist.

EXPLORE A DAYTIME NEIGHBORHOOD AT NIGHT Take a nighttime walk through an explorable area you've already seen by day. You'll get a whole different view of it.

ASK AROUND If you strike up a conversation with like-minded people during the course of your day, ask them about their favorite spots. Your hotel concierge is another resource.

DON'T WING IT As soon as you've nailed down your travel dates, look into local publications or surf the Net to see what's on the calendar while you're in town. Look for hot regional acts, dance and theater, big-name performing artists, expositions, and sporting events. Then call or click to order tickets.

CHECK OUT THE NEIGHBORHOOD Whenever you don't know the neighborhood you'll be visiting, review safety issues with people in your hotel. What's the transportation situation? Can you walk there, or do you need a cab? Is there anything else you need to know?

CASH OR CREDIT? Know before you go. It's always fun to be surprised—but not when you can't cover your check.

CORRAL DE LA MORERÍA. Dinner à la carte and well-known visiting flamenco stars accompany the resident dance troupe. Since Morería opened its doors in 1956, celebrities such as Frank Sinatra and Ava Gardner have left their autographed photos for the walls. Shows are daily, from 10:45 PM to 2 AM. *Morería 17 (on C. Bailén; cross bridge over C. Segovia and turn right), Centro, tel. 91/365–8446.*

LAS CARBONERAS. One of Madrid's prime new flamenco showcases—and less commercial than the traditional and better known tablaos—Las Carboneras presents young artists on their way up as well as more established stars on tour. Shows are staged nightly from 10:30 PM to 2 AM. *Plaza del Conde de Miranda 1, Centro, tel. 91/542–8677.*

Theater

English-language plays are rare. When they do come to town, they're staged at any of a dozen venues. One theater you won't need Spanish for is the **TEATRO DE LA ZARZUELA** (Jovellanos 4, Centro, tel. 91/524–5400), which specializes in the traditional Spanish operetta known as *zarzuela*, a kind of bawdy comedy. The **TEATRO ESPAÑOL** (Príncipe 25, Santa Ana, tel. 91/429–6297) keeps 17th-century Spanish classics alive.

In This Chapter

Updated by George Semler

where to stay

THE SPANISH GOVERNMENT RATES HOTELS with one to five stars. While quality is a factor, the rating is technically only an indication of how many facilities the hotel offers. For example, a three-star hotel may be just as comfortable as a four-star hotel but lack a swimming pool.

All hotel entrances are marked with a blue plaque bearing the letter H and the number of stars. The letter R (standing for *residencia*) after the letter H indicates an establishment with no meal service. The designations *fonda* (F), *pensión* (P), *hostal* (Hs), and *casa de huéspedes* (CH) indicate budget accommodations.

Although a single room (*habitación sencilla*) is usually available, singles are often on the small side. Solo travelers might prefer to pay a bit extra for single occupancy of a double room (*habitación doble uso individual*). All hotels we review have private bathrooms unless otherwise noted.

PRICES

Try bargaining at the pricier properties: weekend discounts of up to 30% are widely available. You can also find *hostal* rooms, often on the upper floors of apartment buildings with shared or private baths, for €30 or less. Because these cheap lodgings are often full and don't take reservations, only a few are listed here—you simply have to try your luck door-to-door. Many are in the old city between the Prado and the Puerta del Sol; start your quest around Plaza Santa Ana.

CATEGORY	COST*
$$$$	over €240
$$$	€150–€240
$$	€90–€150
$	under €90

*for a standard double room, excluding tax

LODGING

$$$$ **ORFILA.** This elegant 1886 town house, hidden away in a leafy little
★ residential street not far from Plaza Colón, has every comfort of
a larger hotel in more intimate, personalized surroundings.
Originally the in-town residence of the literary and aristocratic
Gomez-Acebo family, Orfila 6 was an address famous for theater
performances in the late 19th and early 20th centuries. The
restaurant, garden, and tearoom have period furniture while the
guest rooms are draped with striped and floral silks. *Orfila 6,
Chamberí 28010, tel. 91/702–7770, fax 91/702–7772. 28 rooms, 4
suites. Restaurant, in-room VCRs, pool, health club, sauna, bar, meeting
room, parking (fee). AE, DC, MC, V.*

$$$$ **RITZ.** Alfonso XIII, about to marry Queen Victoria's granddaughter,
realized to his dismay that Madrid had no hotel fit for his royal
guests. Thus was born the Ritz, the most exclusive hotel in Spain.
Opened in 1910 by the king himself (who personally supervised
construction), the Ritz is a monument to the Belle Epoque, its
salons furnished with rare antiques, hand-embroidered linens from
Robinson & Cleaver, and handwoven carpets. Rooms are carpeted,
hung with chandeliers, and decorated in pastels. Many have
views of the Prado. The restaurant, Goya, is famous (though
pricey), and Sunday brunch is a lavish feast to the soothing strains
of harp music. Weekend tea and supper are accompanied by
chamber music from February to May. *Plaza de la Lealtad 5, Prado
28014, tel. 91/521–2857, fax 91/701–6776. 158 rooms. Restaurant,
in-room data ports, in-room fax, in-room VCRs, hair salon, health club,
massage, sauna, bar, parking (fee). AE, DC, MC, V.*

$$$$ **SANTO MAURO.** Once the Canadian embassy, this turn-of-the-
★ 20th-century mansion is now an intimate luxury hotel, an oasis
of calm just a 10-minute cab ride from the city center. The
neoclassical architecture is accented by contemporary furniture
in such hues as mustard, teal, and eggplant. The best rooms are
in the main building, as is the top-notch restaurant. Rooms in the
annex are duplexes with stereos and VCRs. Views vary; request a
room with a terrace overlooking the gardens. *Zurbano 36, Chamberí
28010, tel. 91/319–6900, fax 91/308–5477. 37 rooms. Restaurant,
coffee shop, in-room VCRs, pool, gym, sauna, bar, meeting room, parking
(fee). AE, DC, MC, V.*

$$$$ **VILLA MAGNA.** The concrete facade here gives way to an interior
furnished with 18th-century antiques. Prices are robust, but it's
hard to find flourishes such as a champagne bar and—in the
largest suite in Madrid—a white baby-grand piano. All rooms have
large desks as well as VCRs, and all bathrooms have fresh flowers.
One restaurant, Le Divellec, has walnut paneling and the feel of
an English library, and you can dine on its garden terrace in
season. The other restaurant, the Tse-Yang, is Madrid's most
exclusive for Chinese food. *Paseo de la Castellana 22, Salamanca
28046, tel. 91/587–1234, fax 91/431–2286 or 91/575–3158. 164 rooms,
18 suites. 2 restaurants, in-room VCRs, hair salon, health club, massage,
sauna, 2 bars, baby-sitting, business services, car rental, parking (fee). AE,
DC, MC, V.*

$$$$ **VILLA REAL.** For a medium-size hotel that combines elegance,
★ modern amenities, friendly service, and a great location, look no
further: the Villa Real faces Spain's parliament and is convenient
to almost everything, particularly the Prado and Thyssen-
Bornemisza museums. The simulated 19th-century facade gives
way to an intimate lobby garnished with potted palms. Many
rooms are split-level, with a small sitting area. Some suites have
saunas and whirlpool baths. *Plaza de las Cortés 10, Prado 28014, tel.
91/420–3767, fax 91/420–2547. 94 rooms, 20 suites. Restaurant, in-
room data ports, hair salon, sauna, bar, meeting room, parking (fee). AE,
DC, MC, V.*

madrid lodging

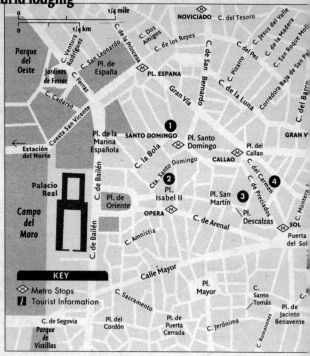

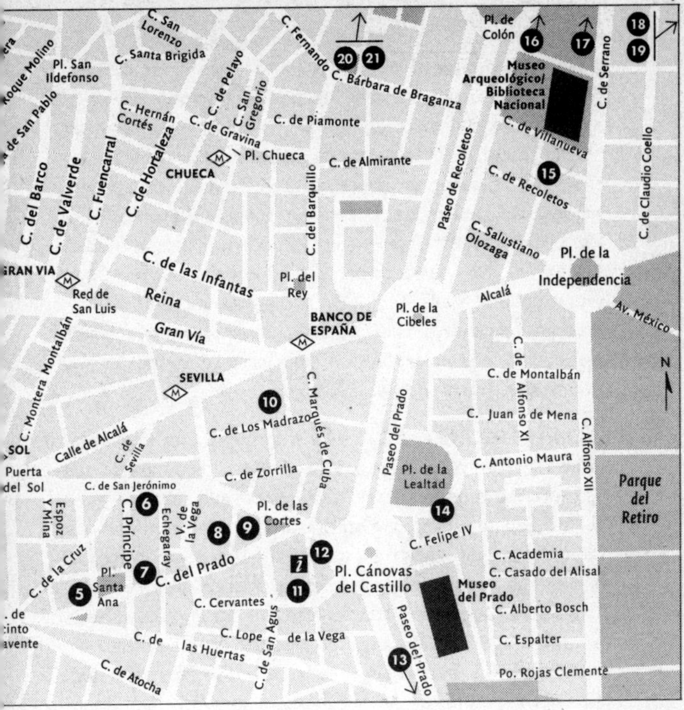

C. San Lorenzo
C. Fernando
Pl. San Ildefonso
C. Santa Brigida
C. de Pelayo
C. San Gregorio
C. Bárbara de Braganza
Pl. de Colón
Museo Arqueológico/ Biblioteca Nacional
C. de Serrano
C. Hernán Cortés
C. de Gravina
C. de Piamonte
C. de Villanueva
Pl. Chueca
C. de Almirante
CHUECA
C. del Barco
C. de Valverde
C. Fuencarral
C. de Hortaleza
C. del Barquillo
Paseo de Recoletos
C. de Recoletos
C. de Claudio Coello
C. Salustiano Olozaga
Pl. de la Independencia
GRAN VIA
C. de las Infantas
Pl. del Rey
Red de San Luis
Reina
Alcalá
Av. México
Pl. de la Cibeles
BANCO DE ESPAÑA
Gran Vía
C. Montera
Montalbán
SEVILLA
C. Marqués de Cuba
C. de Alfonso XI
C. de Montalbán
N
C. Juan de Mena
C. de Los Madrazo
Paseo del Prado
C. Alfonso XII
Calle de Alcalá
C. de Sevilla
SOL
Puerta del Sol
C. de Zorrilla
C. Antonio Maura
Pl. de la Lealtad
Parque del Retiro
C. de San Jerónimo
Espoz Y Mina
C. Príncipe
Echegaray
V. de la Vega
Pl. de las Cortes
C. Felipe IV
C. Academia
C. de la Cruz
C. del Prado
Pl. Cánovas del Castillo
C. Casado del Alisal
Pl. Santa Ana
Museo del Prado
C. Cervantes
C. Alberto Bosch
C. Lope de la Vega
C. de San Agus
C. de las Huertas
C. Espalter
C. de Atocha
Po. Rojas Clemente
5
6
7
8
9
10
11
12
13
14
15
16
17
18
19
20
21

$$$$ WESTIN PALACE. ★ Built in 1912, Madrid's most famous grand hotel is a belle epoque creation of Alfonso XIII and has hosted the likes of Dalí, Brando, Hayworth, and Madonna. Guest rooms are high-tech and generally impeccable; banquet halls and lobbies have been beautified and the facade restored. The art nouveau stained-glass dome over the lounge remains exquisitely original, while guest room windows are double-glazed against street noise. The suites are no less luxurious than the opulent public spaces with Bang & Olufsen CD players, spacious bathrooms, double sinks, hot tubs, and separate shower stalls. *Plaza de las Cortés 7, Prado 28014, tel. 91/360–8000, fax 91/360–8100, www.palacemadrid.com. 465 rooms, 45 suites. 2 restaurants, café, in-room data ports, gym, sauna, bar, business services, meeting room, parking (fee). AE, DC, MC, V.*

$$$ JARDÍN DE RECOLETOS. This sleek apartment hotel offers great value in a quiet street close to Plaza Colón and upmarket Calle Serrano. The large lobby has marble floors and a stained-glass ceiling and adjoins a café and restaurant. The commodious rooms, with light-wood trim, white walls, and beige and yellow furnishings, include sitting and dining areas and well-equipped kitchens. "Superior" rooms and two-room suites have hydromassage baths and large terraces. Book well in advance. *Gil de Santivañes 6, Salamanca 28001, tel. 91/781–1640, fax 91/781–1641. 36 rooms, 7 suites. Restaurant, café, in-room data ports, kitchenettes, in-room VCRs, parking (fee). AE, DC, MC, V.*

$$$ NH LAGASCA. In the heart of the elegant Salamanca neighborhood, this newish hotel combines large, brightly decorated rooms with an unbeatable location two blocks from Madrid's main shopping street, Calle Serrano. The marble lobbies border on the coldly functional, but they're fine as a meeting place. *Lagasca 64, Salamanca 28001, tel. 91/575–4606, fax 91/575–1694. 100 rooms. Restaurant, in-room VCRs, bar, meeting room, parking (fee). AE, DC, MC, V.*

$$$ TRYP AMBASSADOR. ★ On an old street between Gran Vía and the Royal Palace, the Ambassador is in the renovated 19th-century

Find America *with a Compass*

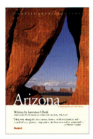
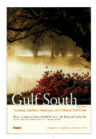
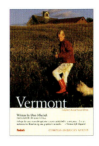

Written by local authors and illustrated throughout
with spectacular color images, the Compass American
Guides reveal the character and culture of more than
40 of America's most fascinating destinations. Perfect
for residents who want to explore their own backyard,
and visitors who want an insider's perspective on
the history, heritage, and all there is to see and do.

Fodor's COMPASS AMERICAN GUIDES

At bookstores everywhere.

When you pack your MCI Calling Card, it's like packing your loved ones along too.

Your MCI Calling Card is the easy way to stay in touch when you travel. Use it to call to and from over 125 countries. Plus, every time you call, you can earn frequent flier miles. So wherever your travels take you, call home with your MCI Calling Card. It's even easy to get one. Just visit **www.mci.com/worldphone** or **www.mci.com/partners**.

EASY TO CALL WORLDWIDE
1. Just enter the WorldPhone® access number of the country you're calling from.
2. Enter or give the operator your MCI Calling Card number.
3. Enter or give the number you're calling.

		Ireland	1-800-55-1001
Australia ◆	1-800-881-100	Italy ◆	800-17-2401
China	108-12	Japan ◆	00539-121▶
France ◆	0-800-99-0019	South Africa	0800-99-0011
Germany	0800-888-8000	Spain	900-99-0014
Hong Kong	800-96-1121	United Kingdom	0800-89-0222

◆ Public phones may require deposit of coin or phone card for dial tone. ▶ Regulation does not permit intra-Japan calls.

EARN FREQUENT FLIER MILES

palace of the Dukes of Granada. A magnificent front door and a graceful three-story staircase recall the building's aristocratic past; the rest has been transformed into elegant, somewhat soulless lodgings favored by executives. Large guest rooms have sitting areas and mahogany furnishings, floral drapes, and bedspreads. The greenhouse restaurant, filled with plants and songbirds, is especially pleasant on cold days. *Cuesta Santo Domingo 5 and 7, Opera 28013, tel. 91/541–6700, fax 91/559–1040, www.tryp.es. 181 rooms. Restaurant, bar, airport shuttle, parking (fee). AE, DC, MC, V.*

\$\$\$ TRYP FÉNIX. A magnificent marble lobby greets your arrival at this Madrid institution, overlooking Plaza de Colón on the Castellana. The Fenix is also a mere hop from the posh shops of Calle Serrano. Its spacious rooms, decorated in reds and golds, are carpeted and amply furnished, and flowers abound. Ask for a room facing the Plaza de Colón; otherwise, the view is rather dreary. *Hermosilla 2, Salamanca 28001, tel. 91/431–6700, fax 91/576–0661. 213 rooms, 12 suites. Café, hair salon, bar, baby-sitting, parking (fee). AE, DC, MC, V.*

\$\$–\$\$\$ REINA VICTORIA. Long a Madrid favorite, particularly with bullfighters, this gleaming white Victorian building across Plaza Santa Ana from the Teatro Español was modernized at the end of the 20th century. The taurine theme is most evident in the bar, where stuffed bulls' heads peer curiously over your shoulder. The best rooms are the highest, for both the quiet and the views over the rooftops or theater. On Friday and Saturday nights it can be impossible to escape the street noise below, and the coffee in the breakfast room should be avoided at all costs. *Plaza Santa Ana 14, Santa Ana 28012, tel. 91/531–4500, fax 91/522–0307. 195 rooms. Bar, meeting rooms. AE, DC, MC, V.*

\$\$–\$\$\$ SANTO DOMINGO. An intimate hotel that blends the best of classical and modern design, the Santo Domingo is about 10 minutes' walk from the Puerta del Sol, just off Gran Vía. Rooms are done in soft tones of peach and ocher, and those on the fifth floor have views of the Royal Palace. All have voice mail and double-paned windows. A friendly staff gives the place a personal touch. *Plaza Santo*

Domingo 13, Sol 28013, tel. 91/547–9800, fax 91/547–5995. 120 rooms. Restaurant, bar, meeting room, parking (fee). AE, DC, MC, V.

$$–$$$ SUECIA. The Suecia's chief attraction is its location, right next to the super-chic Círculo de Bellas Artes (an arts society–café–film–theater complex). The large lobby, which includes a café, is often bustling. Guest rooms are trendy, with contemporary art and futuristic light fixtures, but a little worn. *Marqués de Riera 4, Santa Ana 28014, tel. 91/531–6900, fax 91/521–7141. 119 rooms, 9 suites. 2 restaurants, bar, baby-sitting, parking (fee). AE, DC, MC, V.*

$$–$$$ SUITE PRADO. Popular with Americans on short stays, this stylish apartment hotel is near the Prado, the Thyssen-Bornemisza, and the Plaza Santa Ana tapas area. The attractive attic studios on the fifth floor have sloping, beamed ceilings, and there are larger suites downstairs. All apartments are brightly decorated and have marble baths and basic kitchens, but breakfast is served by the friendly staff on weekends. *Manuel Fernández y González 10, Santa Ana 28014, tel. 91/420–2318, fax 91/420–0559. 18 suites. Kitchenettes, parking (fee). AE, DC, MC, V.*

$$ EL PRADO. Wedged between the classic buildings of *castizo* Madrid, this skinny hotel is within stumbling distance of the city's best bars and nightclubs and is priced accordingly. Rooms are basic but spacious and virtually immune to street noise thanks to double-pane windows. Decorative touches include pastel floral prints and gleaming marble baths. *C. Prado 11, Santa Ana 28014, tel. 91/369–0234, fax 91/429–2829. 47 rooms. Cafeteria, meeting room, parking (fee). AE, DC, MC, V.*

$$ LIABENY. A large, paneled lobby leads to bars, a restaurant, and a café in this 1960s hotel, near a plaza (and several department stores) between Gran Vía and Puerta del Sol. The large rooms have floral fabrics and big windows; interior and top-floor rooms are the quietest. *Salud 3, Sol 28013, tel. 91/531–9000, fax 91/532–5306. 222 rooms. Restaurant, café, 2 bars, meeting room, parking (fee). AE, DC, MC, V.*

$–$$ CARLOS V. If you like to be in the center of things, hang your hat at this classic hotel on a pedestrian street a few steps from the Puerta del Sol, Plaza Mayor, and Descalzas Reales convent, and the price is right. A suit of armor decorates the tiny lobby, while crystal chandeliers add elegance to the second-floor guest lounge. All rooms are bright and carpeted, and the doubles with large terraces are a bargain. *Maestro Victoria 5, Sol 28013, tel. 91/531–4100, fax 91/ 531–3761. 67 rooms, 41 with bath. Bar, airport shuttle. AE, DC, MC, V.*

$ HOSTAL DULCINEA. Run by an elderly Spanish couple (who also own the Hostal Corbero, across the street), the Dulcinea is a friendly, clean, and affordable alternative to the pricey hotels on Paseo del Prado. Just off the Plaza Cánovas del Castillo, this upper-floor pension has an arguably ideal location: it's surrounded by the Museo Thyssen-Bornemisza to the north, the Prado to the east, and the vibrant nightlife around the Plaza Santa Ana to the west. Rooms are spare, with wood furniture and minimal trimmings, but comfortable and homey. Calling ahead can get you a great price on one of the three cozy "apartments." *Cervantes 19, Santa Ana 28014, tel. 91/429–9309, fax 91/369–2569. 23 rooms, 3 apartments. AE, MC, V.*

$ INGLÉS. Virginia Woolf was among the first luminaries to discover this place, which is smack in the middle of the old city's bar-and-restaurant district. Since Woolf's time, the Inglés has attracted more than its share of less-celebrated artists and writers. Rather drab and deteriorated now, it's best for those looking for location and value rather than luxury. (Run-down suites cost what you'd pay for a standard double.) The balconies overlooking Calle Echegaray give you an unusual aerial view of the medieval quarter, all red tiles and ramshackle gables. *Echegaray 8, Santa Ana 28014, tel. 91/429–6551, fax 91/420–2423. 58 rooms. Cafeteria, gym, bar, parking (fee). AE, DC, MC, V.*

$ MORA. Across the Paseo del Prado from the Botanical Garden, ★ the Mora welcomes weary travelers with a sparkling, faux-marble lobby and bright, carpeted hallways. Guest rooms are modestly

Hotel How-Tos

Where you stay does make a difference. Do you prefer a modern high-rise or an intimate B&B? A center-city location or the quiet suburbs? What facilities do you want? Sort through your priorities, then price it all out.

HOW TO GET A DEAL After you've chosen a likely candidate or two, phone them directly and price a room for your travel dates. Then call the hotel's toll-free number and ask the same questions. Also try consolidators and hotel-room discounters. You won't hear the same rates twice. On the spot, make a reservation as soon as you are quoted a price you want to pay.

PROMISES, PROMISES If you have special requests, make them when you reserve. Get written confirmation of any promises.

SETTLE IN Upon arriving, make sure everything works—lights and lamps, TV and radio, sink, tub, shower, and anything else that matters. Report any problems immediately. And don't wait until you need extra pillows or blankets or an ironing board to call housekeeping. Also check out the fire emergency instructions. Know where to find the fire exits, and make sure your companions do, too.

IF YOU NEED TO COMPLAIN Be polite but firm. Explain the problem to the person in charge. Suggest a course of action. If you aren't satisfied, repeat your requests to the manager. Document everything: Take pictures and keep a written record of who you've spoken with, when, and what was said. Contact your travel agent, if he made the reservations.

KNOW THE SCORE When you go out, take your hotel's business cards (one for everyone in your party). If you have extras, you can give them out to new acquaintances who want to call you.

TIP UP FRONT For special services, a tip or partial tip in advance can work wonders.

USE ALL THE HOTEL RESOURCES A concierge can make difficult things easy. But a desk clerk, bellhop, or other hotel employee who's friendly, smart, and ambitious can often steer you straight as well. A gratuity is in order if the advice is helpful.

decorated but large and comfortable; those on the street side have great views of the gardens and the Prado, and double-pane windows keep them fairly quiet. For breakfast and lunch, the attached café is excellent, affordable, and popular with locals. *Paseo del Prado 32, Centro 28014, tel. 91/420–1569, fax 91/420–0564. 60 rooms. Café. AE, DC, MC, V.*

$ **RAMÓN DE LA CRUZ.** If you don't mind a 10-minute metro ride (to Manuel Becerra) from the city center, this medium-size hotel is a find. Rooms are large, with modern bathrooms, and the stone-floor lobby is spacious. *Don Ramón de la Cruz 94, Salamanca 28006, tel. 91/401–7200, fax 91/402–2126. 103 rooms. Cafeteria. MC, V.*

In This Chapter

Updated by George Semler

side trips

MADRID'S SOPHISTICATION STANDS in vivid contrast to the ancient ways of the historic towns nearby. Less than an hour from downtown are villages whose farm fields may still be plowed by mules. Like urbanites the world over, Madrileños chill out in the countryside, so getaways to the dozens of Castilian hamlets nearby are cherished by travelers and locals alike.

Numbers in the margins correspond to numbers on the Side Trips from Madrid and El Escorial maps.

EL ESCORIAL
50 km (31 mi) northwest of Madrid.

Felipe II was one of history's most deeply religious and forbidding monarchs—not to mention one of its most powerful—and the great granite monastery that he had constructed in a remarkable 21 years (1563–84) is an enduring testament to his character. Outside Madrid in the foothills of the Sierra de Guadarrama, the **REAL MONASTERIO DE SAN LORENZO DE EL ESCORIAL** (Royal Monastery of St. Lawrence of Escorial) is severe, rectilinear, and unforgiving—one of the most gigantic yet simple architectural monuments on the Iberian Peninsula.

Felipe built the monastery in the village of San Lorenzo de El Escorial to commemorate Spain's crushing victory over the French at Saint-Quentin on August 10, 1557, and as a final resting place for his all-powerful father, the Holy Roman

Emperor Carlos V. He filled the place with treasures as he ruled the largest empire the world has ever seen, knowing all the while that a marble coffin awaited him in the pantheon deep below. The building's vast rectangle, encompassing 16 courts, is modeled on the red-hot grille upon which St. Lawrence was martyred—appropriate enough, since August 10 was that saint's day. (It's also said that Felipe's troops accidentally destroyed a church dedicated to St. Lawrence during the battle and he sought to make amends.) Some years ago a Spanish psychohistorian theorized that the building is shaped like a prone woman and is thus an unintended emblem of Felipe's sexual repression. Lo and behold, this thesis provoked several newspaper articles and a rash of other commentary.

El Escorial is easily reached by car, train, bus, or organized tour from Madrid; simply inquire at a travel agency or the appropriate station. The building and its adjuncts—a palace, museum, church, and more—can take hours or even days to tour. Easter Sunday's candelit midnight mass draws crowds, as does the summer tourist season.

The monastery was begun by Juan Bautista de Toledo but finished in 1584 by Juan de Herrera, who would eventually give his name to a major Spanish architectural school. It was completed just in time for Felipe to die here, gangrenous and tortured by the gout that had plagued him for years, in the tiny, sparsely furnished bedroom that resembled a monk's cell more than the resting place of a great monarch. It is in this bedroom—which looks out, through a private entrance, into the royal chapel—that you most appreciate the man's spartan nature. Spain's later Bourbon kings, such as Carlos III and Carlos IV, had clearly different tastes, and their apartments, connected to Felipe's by the Hall of Battles, are far more luxurious.

Perhaps the most interesting part of the entire Escorial is the **Panteón de los Reyes** (Royal Pantheon), which contains the body of every king since Carlos I save three—Felipe V (buried at La Granja), Ferdinand VI (in Madrid), and Amadeus of Savoy (in Italy). The body of Alfonso XIII, who died in Rome in 1941, was brought to El Escorial in January 1980. The rulers' bodies lie in 26 sumptuous marble and bronze sarcophagi that line the walls (three of which are empty, awaiting future rulers). Only those queens who bore sons later crowned lie in the same crypt; the others, along with royal sons and daughters who never ruled, lie

el escorial

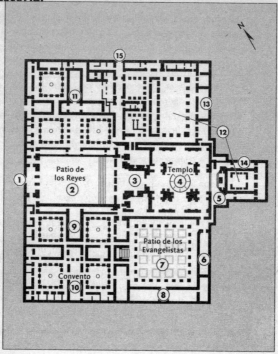

Apartments of Philip II, 14	Convento, 10	Patio de los Reyes (Court of the Kings), 2	Stairway to Panteón de los Reyes (Royal Pantheon), 5
Basilica, 4	Main Entrance, 1	Royal Palace, 12	
Biblioteca (Library), 9	Museum, 13	Sacristy, 6	Tour Entrance, 15
Choir, 3	Patio de los Evangelistas (Court of the Evangelists), 7	Salas Capitulares (Chapter Houses), 8	
Colegio, 11			

nearby, in the **Panteón de los Infantes.** Many of the royal children are in a single circular tomb made of Carrara marble.

Another highlight is the monastery's surprisingly lavish and colorful **library,** with ceiling paintings by Michelangelo disciple Pellegrino Tibaldi (1527–96). The imposing austerity of El Escorial's facades makes this chromatic explosion especially powerful; try to save it for last. The library houses 50,000 rare manuscripts, codices, and ancient books, including the diary of St. Teresa of Ávila and the gold-lettered, illuminated Codex Aureus. Tapestries woven from cartoons by Goya, Rubens, and El Greco cover almost every inch of wall space in huge sections of the building, and extraordinary canvases by Velázquez, El Greco, David, Ribera, Tintoretto, Rubens, and other masters, collected from around the monastery, are now displayed in the **Museos Nuevos** (New Museums). In the **basilica,** don't miss the fresco above the choir, depicting heaven, or Titian's fresco *The Martyrdom of St. Lawrence,* which shows the saint being roasted alive. *San Lorenzo de El Escorial, tel. 91/890–5905. €6, guided tour €7. Apr.–Sept., Tues.–Sun. 10–6; Oct.–Mar., Tues.–Sun. 10–5.*

NEED A BREAK? Many Madrileños find El Escorial the perfect place for an enormous weekend lunch. Topping the list of eating spots is the outdoor terrace at **CHAROLÉS** (Floridablanca 24, tel. 91/890–5975), where imaginative seasonal specialties round out a menu of northern-Spanish favorites, such as *bacalao al pil-pil* (salt cod cooked in oil and garlic at a low temperature) and grilled *chuleta* (steak). Just don't expect picnic prices.

VALLE DE LOS CAÍDOS

48 *13 km (8 mi) north of El Escorial on C600.*

Ranked as a not-to-be-missed visit until the death of Generalísimo Francisco Franco in 1975, this massive monument to fascisms's victory over democracy in the 1936–39 Spanish

Civil War (Catholicism's victory over Communism to some) has become something of an anachronism in the modern democratic Spain of today. Now relegated to rallying point for the extreme right on key dates such as the July 18 commemoration of the military uprising of 1936 or the November 20 death of Franco, the Valley of the Fallen is just a few minutes north of El Escorial. A lovely pine forest leads up to a massive basilica carved out of a solid granite mountain. Topped with a cross nearly 500 ft high (accessible by elevator), the basilica holds the tombs of both General Franco and José Antonio Primo de Rivera, founder of the fascist Spanish Falange. It was built with the forced labor of postwar Republican prisoners and dedicated, rather disingenuously, to all who died in the three-year conflict. Tapestries of the Apocalypse add to the generally terrifying air inside as every footstep resounds off the polished marble floors and stone walls. An eerie midnight mass is held here on Easter Sunday, the granite peak lit by candlelight. *tel. 91/890–5611. Basilica €5. Apr.–Sept., Tues.–Sun. 10–7; Oct.–Mar., Tues.–Sun. 10–6.*

CHINCHÓN

49 *54 km (33 mi) southeast of Madrid, off N-III on C300.*

A true Castilian town, the picturesque village of Chinchón seems a good four centuries removed. It makes an ideal day trip, especially if you save time for lunch at one of its many rustic restaurants; the only problem is that swarms of Madrileños have the same idea, so it's often hard to get a table at lunchtime on weekends.

The high point of Chinchón is its charming **PLAZA MAYOR**, an uneven circle of ancient three- and four-story houses embellished with wooden balconies resting on granite columns. It's something like an open-air Elizabethan theater, but with a Spanish flavor—in fact, the entire plaza is converted to a bullring from time to time, with temporary bleachers erected in the center and seats on the privately owned balconies rented out for splendid views. (Tickets for these rare fights are hard to come by.)

The commanding **IGLESIA DE LA ASUNCIÓN** (Church of the Assumption), overlooking the plaza, is known for its Goya mural, *The Assumption of the Virgin*.

Along the C300 near the N-III highway, you'll pass through the **VALLE DEL JARAMA**, scene of one of the bloodiest battles of the Spanish Civil War. American volunteers in the Abraham Lincoln Brigade, which fought with the democratically elected Spanish Republican government against Franco's military insurgency, were mauled here in a baptism of fire. Folk singer Pete Seeger immortalized the battle with "There's a valley in Spain called Jarama. . . ." The trenches are still visible, and bits of rusty military hardware can still be found in the fields.

Dining

The town's arcaded plaza is ringed by charming balconied restaurants serving hearty Castilian fare, particularly roasts and charcoal-grilled meat. Wherever you dine, try the local *anís*, a licorice-flavor spirit; and if you come to Chinchón in April, look for merriment occasioned by the Fiesta del Anís y del Vino (Anise and Wine Festival). On winter weekends, Madrileños in droves come for the superb cocido at the **PARADOR DE CHINCHÓN** (Av. Generalísimo 1, tel. 91/894–0836). **MESÓN DE LA VIRREINA** (Plaza Mayor 28, tel. 91/894–0015), on the square's northeast corner, is a perfect perch for sipping gazpacho or a glass of Chinchón anís. Call ahead for a table at **CAFÉ DE LA IBERIA** (Plaza Mayor 17, tel. 91/894–0998), which has a balcony as well as a cozy interior. **MESÓN LAS CUEVAS DEL VINO** (Benito Hortelano 13, tel. 91/894–0206) is a rambling tavern with roaring fireplaces and immense antique wine and olive-oil amphoras scattered around a giant olive press.

MONASTERIO DE EL PAULAR AND LOZOYA VALLEY

50 100 km (62 mi) north of Madrid.

Rising from Spain's great central *meseta* (plain), the Sierra de Guadarrama looms northwest of Madrid like a dark, jagged shield separating Old and New Castile. Snowcapped for much of the year, the mountains are indeed rough-hewn in many spots, particularly on their northern face, but there is a dramatic exception—the Lozoya Valley.

About 100 km (62 mi) north of the capital, this valley of pines, poplars, and babbling brooks is a cool, green retreat from the often searing heat of the plain. Madrileños repair here for a picnic or a simple drive, rarely joined by foreign travelers, to whom the area is virtually unknown.

You'll need a car to make this trip, and the drive is a pleasant one. Take the A6 northwest from Madrid and exit at signs for the Navacerrada Pass on the N601. As you climb toward the 6,100-ft mountain pass, you'll come to a road bearing off to the left toward Cercedilla. (This little village, a popular base for hikes, is also accessible by train.) Just above Cercedilla, an old Roman road leads up to the ridge of the Guadarrama, where an ancient fountain, known as Fuenfría, long provided the spring water that fed the Roman aqueduct of Segovia. The path traced by this cobble road is very close to the route Hemingway had his hero Robert Jordan take in *For Whom the Bell Tolls* and eventually takes you near the bridge that Jordan blew up in the novel.

If you continue past the Cercedilla road, you'll come to a ski resort at the highest point of the Navacerrada Pass. Take a right here on C604 and you'll follow the ridge of the mountains for a few miles before descending into the **LOZOYA VALLEY**. The valley is filled with picnic spots along the Lozoya River, including several campgrounds. To end the excursion, take C604 north a few miles to Rascafría, and then turn right on a smaller road marked for Miraflores de la Sierra. In that town you'll turn right again, following signs for Colmenar Viejo, and then pick up a short expressway back to Madrid.

Built by King Juan I in 1390, **MONASTERIO DE EL PAULAR** (tel. 91/869–1425) was the first Carthusian monastery in Castile, but it has been neglected since the Disentailment of 1836, when religious organizations gave their artistic treasures to the state. Fewer than a dozen Benedictine monks still live here, eating and praying exactly as their predecessors did centuries ago. One of them gives tours every day but Thursday at noon, 1, and 5. The monastery is on your left as you approach the floor of the Lozoya Valley. The monastery is attached to **Santa María de El Paular** (tel. 91/869–1011, fax 91/869–1006), a cozy mountain refuge run by the same Westin chain that owns the hotel Palace.

practical information

Air Travel

CARRIERS

From North America, American, Continental, US Airways, Air Europa, Spanair, and TWA fly to Madrid; American, Delta, and Iberia fly to Madrid and Barcelona. Within Spain, Iberia is the main domestic airline, but Air Europa and Spanair fly domestic routes at lower prices. Iberia runs a shuttle, the *puente aereo*, between Madrid and Barcelona from around 7 AM to 11 PM; planes depart hourly and more frequently in the morning and afternoon commute hours. You don't need to reserve ahead; you can buy your tickets at the airport ticket counter upon arriving. Terminal C in the Barcelona airport is used exclusively by the shuttle; in Madrid, the shuttle departs from Terminal 3. The Spanish predilection for cigarettes notwithstanding, most airlines serving Spain, including Iberia, don't allow smoking on international or domestic flights.

➤FROM NORTH AMERICA: Air Europa (tel. 888/238–7672). American (tel. 800/433–7300). Continental (tel. 800/231–0856). Delta (tel. 800/221–1212). Iberia (tel. 800/772–4642). Spanair (tel. 888/545–5757). TWA (tel. 800/892–4141). US Airways (tel. 800/622–1015).

➤FROM THE U.K.: British Airways (tel. 0845/773–3377). EasyJet (tel. 0870/600–0000). Go (tel. 0870/607–6543). Iberia (tel. 0845/601–2854).

➤**WITHIN SPAIN: Air Europa** (tel. 902/401501). **Iberia** (902/400500). **Spanair** (tel. 902/131415).

CHECK-IN AND BOARDING

Always ask your carrier about its check-in policy. Plan to arrive at the airport about 1½ hours before your scheduled departure time for domestic flights and 2½ to 3 hours before international flights.

FLYING TIMES

Flying time from New York is seven hours; from London, just over two.

➤**AIRPORTS:** Madrid is served by Madrid Barajas Airport, 12 km (7 mi) east of the city.

➤**INFORMATION: Aeropuerto de Madrid Barajas** (tel. 91/305–8343, 91/305–8344, 91/305–8345, or 91/393–6000).

Airport Transfers

The speediest transfer is the Line 8 metro, running every few minutes (daily from 6:30 AM to 10:30 PM) between Nuevos Ministerios and Barajas Airport; it's €1 and takes 12 minutes.

For a mere €3 there's a convenient bus to the central Plaza Colón, where you can catch a taxi to your hotel. Buses leave every 15 minutes between 5:40 AM and 2 AM (slightly less often very early or late in the day). Watch your belongings, as the underground Plaza Colón bus station is a favorite haunt of purse snatchers and con artists.

In bad traffic, the 15-minute taxi ride to Madrid can take the better part of an hour, but it makes sense if you have a lot of luggage. Taxis normally wait outside the airport terminal near the clearly marked bus stop; expect to pay up to €15, more in heavy traffic, plus small holiday, late-night, and/or luggage surcharges. Make sure the driver is on the meter—off-the-meter "deals" almost always cost more. Finally, some hotels offer shuttle service in vans; check with yours when you reserve.

Business Hours

BANKS AND OFFICES

Banks are generally open Monday–Friday 8:30 or 9 until 2 or 2:30. Some banks occasionally open on Saturday 8:30 or 9 until 2 or 2:30. From October to May, savings banks are also open Thursday 4:30–8. Currency exchanges at airports and train stations stay open later; you can also cash traveler's checks at El Corte Inglés department stores until 10 PM (some branches close at 9 PM or 9:30 PM.) Most government offices are open weekdays 9–2 only.

MUSEUMS AND SIGHTS

Most museums are open from 9:30 to 2 and 4 to 7 six days a week, usually every day but Monday. Schedules are subject to change, particularly between the high and low seasons, so **confirm opening hours before you make plans.** A few large museums, such as Madrid's Prado and Reina Sofía and Barcelona's Picasso Museum, stay open all day, without a siesta.

PHARMACIES

Pharmacies keep normal business hours (9–1:30 and 5–8), but every mid-size town (or city neighborhood) has a duty pharmacy that stays open 24 hours. The location of the duty pharmacy is usually posted on the front door of all pharmacies.

SHOPS

When planning a shopping trip, remember that **almost all shops in Spain close at midday** for at least three hours. The only exceptions are large supermarkets and the department-store chain El Corte Inglés. Stores are generally open from 9 or 10 to 1:30 and from 5 to 8. Most shops are closed on Sunday, and in Madrid and several other places they're also closed Saturday afternoon. Larger shops in tourist areas may stay open Sunday in summer and during the Christmas holiday.

Bus Travel to and from Madrid

Madrid has no central bus station; buses are generally less popular than trains (though they can be faster). Most of southern Spain is served by the Estación del Sur. Buses for much of the rest of the peninsula, including Cuenca, Extremadura, Salamanca, and Valencia, depart from the Auto Res station. There are several smaller stations, however, so inquire at travel agencies for the one serving your destination.

Bus companies of interest include La Sepulvedana, serving Segovia, Ávila, and La Granja; Herranz, for El Escorial and the Valle de los Caídos; Continental Auto, serving Cantabria and the Basque region; and La Veloz, with service to Chinchón.

►**BUS COMPANIES: Continental Auto** (C. Alenza 20, Chamartín, tel. 902–33–04–00; metro: Ríos Rosas). **Herranz** (Fernández de los Ríos s/n, Moncloa, tel. 91/730–9678; metro: Moncloa). **La Sepulvedana** (Paseo de la Florida 11, near Estación del Norte, Moncloa, tel. 91/530–4800). **La Veloz** (Mediterraneo 49, Atocha, tel. 91/409–7602; metro: Conde de Casal).

►**BUS STATIONS: Auto Res** (Plaza Conde de Casal 6, Atocha; metro: Conde de Casal). **Estación del Sur** (Méndez Álvaro s/n, Atocha, tel. 91/468–4200; metro: Méndez Álvaro).

Bus Travel within Madrid

Red city buses run between 6 AM and midnight and cost €1 per ride. After midnight, buses called *buyos* ("night owls") run out to the suburbs from Plaza de Cibeles for the same price. Signs at every stop list all other stops by street name, but they're hard to comprehend if you don't know the city well. Pick up a free route map from EMT kiosks on the Plaza de Cibeles or the Puerta del Sol, where you can also buy a 10-ride ticket called a Metrobus (€5) that's valid for the metro. If you speak Spanish, call for information (tel. 91/406–8810). Drivers will generally make change for anything up to a €10 note. If you've bought a 10-ride ticket, step just behind the driver and insert it in the ticket-punching machine until the mechanism rings.

Car Rental

Avis, Hertz, Budget, and National (partnered in Spain with the Spanish agency Atesa) have branches at major Spanish airports and in large cities. Smaller, regional companies offer lower rates. All agencies have a range of models, but virtually all cars in Spain have a manual transmission—**if you don't want a stick shift, reserve weeks in advance and specify automatic transmission,** then call to reconfirm your automatic car before you leave for Spain. Rates in Madrid begin at the equivalents of U.S. $65 a day and $300 a week for an economy car with air-conditioning, manual transmission, and unlimited mileage. Add to this a 16% tax on car rentals. While you should always rent the size car that makes you feel safest, a small car, aside from saving you money, is prudent for the tiny roads and parking spaces in many parts of Spain.

➤MAJOR AGENCIES: **Alamo** (tel. 800/522–9696, www.alamo. com). **Avis** (tel. 800/331–1084; 800/879–2847 in Canada; 0870/ 606–0100 in the U.K.; 02/9353–9000 in Australia; 09/526–2847 in New Zealand; www.avis.com). **Budget** (tel. 800/527–0700; 0870/156–5656 in the U.K.; www.budget.com). **Dollar** (tel. 800/ 800–6000; 0124/622–0111 in the U.K., where it's affiliated with Sixt; 02/9223–1444 in Australia; www.dollar.com). **Hertz** (tel. 800/654–3001; 800/263–0600 in Canada; 020/8897–2072 in the U.K.; 02/9669–2444 in Australia; 09/256–8690 in New Zealand; www.hertz.com). **National Car Rental** (tel. 800/227–7368; 020/ 8680–4800 in the U.K.; www.nationalcar.com).

➤LOCAL AGENCIES: **Avis** (tel. 902/135531). **Budget** (tel. 901/ 201212). **Europcar** (tel. 902/105030). **Hertz** (tel. 902/402405). **National/Atesa** (tel. 902/100101).

REQUIREMENTS AND RESTRICTIONS

Your own driver's license is valid in Spain, but you may want to get an International Driver's Permit for extra assurance, as having one may save you a problem with local authorities. Permits are available from the American or Canadian Automobile Association, or, in the United Kingdom, from the Automobile Association or Royal Automobile Club. Note that while anyone over 18 with a valid license can drive in Spain, some rental agencies will not rent cars to drivers under 21.

SURCHARGES

Before you pick up a car in one city and leave it in another, **ask about drop-off charges or one-way service fees,** which can be substantial. Note, too, that some rental agencies charge extra if you return the car before the time specified in your contract. To avoid a hefty refueling fee, **fill the tank just before you turn in the car,** but be aware that gas stations near the rental outlet may overcharge. It's almost never a deal to buy the tank of gas in the car when you rent it; the understanding is that you'll return it empty, but some fuel usually remains.

Car Travel

Felipe II made Madrid the capital of Spain because it was at the very center of his peninsular domains, and to this day many of the nation's highways radiate from Madrid like the spokes of a wheel. Originating at Kilometer 0—marked by a brass plaque on the sidewalk of the Puerta del Sol—these highways include the A6 (Segovia, Salamanca, Galicia); A1 (Burgos and the Basque Country); the N-II (Guadalajara, Barcelona, France); the N-III (Cuenca, Valencia, the Mediterranean coast); the A4 (Aranjuez, La Mancha, Granada, Seville); the N401 (Toledo); and the N-V (Talavera de la Reina, Portugal). The city is surrounded by the M30 (the inner ring road) and M40 (the outer ring road), from which most of these highways are easily picked up. Driving in Madrid is best avoided. Parking is nightmarish, traffic is heavy almost all the time, and the city's daredevil drivers can be frightening. August is an exception; the streets are then largely emptied by the mass exodus of Madrileños on vacation.

Driving is the best way to see Spain's rural areas. The main cities are connected by a network of excellent four-lane *autovías* (freeways) and *autopistas* (toll freeways; "toll" is *peaje*), which are designated with the letter A and have speed limits of up to 120 kph (74 mph). The letter N indicates a *carretera nacional* (basic national route), which may have four or two lanes. Smaller towns and villages are connected by a network of secondary roads maintained by regional, provincial, and local governments. Spain's major routes bear heavy traffic, especially holidays. Drive with care: the roads are shared by a potentially perilous mixture of local drivers, Moroccan immigrants traveling between North Africa and northern Europe, and non-Spanish vacationers, some of whom are accustomed to driving on the left side of the road. Be prepared, too, for heavy truck traffic on national routes, which, in the case of two-lane roads, can have you creeping along for hours.

➤LOCAL AUTO CLUBS: RACE (José Abascal 10, Madrid, tel. 900/200093).

EMERGENCY SERVICES

The rental agencies Hertz and Avis have 24-hour breakdown service. If you belong to an auto club (AAA, CAA, or AA), you can get emergency assistance from the Spanish counterpart, RACE (☞ Local Auto Clubs).

GASOLINE

Gas stations are plentiful, and most of those on major routes and in big cities are open 24 hours. On less-traveled routes, gas stations are usually open 7 AM–11 PM. If a gas station is closed, it's required by law that it post the address and directions to the nearest open station. Most stations are self-service, though prices are the same as those at full-service stations. You punch in the amount of gas you want (in Euros, not in liters), unhook the nozzle, pump the gas, and then pay. At night, however, you must pay before you fill up. Most pumps offer a choice of gas, including leaded, unleaded, and diesel, so **be careful to pick the right one** for your car. All newer cars in Spain use *gasolina sin plomo* (unleaded gas), which is available in two grades, 95 and 98 octane. *Super*, regular 97-octane leaded gas, is gradually being phased out. Prices vary little among stations and were at press time €.82 a liter for leaded, 97 octane; €.76 a liter for *sin plomo* (unleaded; 95 octane), and €.89 a liter for unleaded, 98 octane. Credit cards are widely accepted.

RULES OF THE ROAD

Spaniards drive on the right. Horns are banned in cities, but that doesn't keep people from blasting away. Children under 10 may not ride in the front seat, and seat belts are compulsory everywhere. Speed limits are 50 kph (31 mph) in cities, 100 kph (62 mph) on N roads, 120 kph (74 mph) on the *autopista* or *autovía*, and, unless otherwise signposted, 90 kph (56 mph) on other roads. Spanish highway police are particularly vigilant about speeding and illegal passing. Fines start at €90, and police are empowered to demand payment from non-Spanish drivers on the spot. Although local drivers, especially in cities like Madrid, will park their cars just about anywhere, you should **park only in legal spots.** Parking fines are steep, and your car might well be towed, resulting in fines, hassle, and wasted time.

Children in Spain

Children are greatly indulged in Spain. You'll see kids accompanying their parents everywhere, including bars and restaurants. Shopkeepers often offer kids *caramelos* (sweets), and even the coldest waiters tend to be friendlier when you have a youngster with you, and you won't be shunted into a remote corner. However, you won't find high chairs, or children's menus; kids are expected to eat what their parents do, so it's perfectly acceptable to ask for an extra plate and share your food. Be prepared for late bedtimes, especially in summer—it's common to see toddlers playing cheerfully outdoors until midnight. Because children are expected to be with their parents at all times, few hotels provide baby-sitting services; but those that don't can often refer you to an independent baby-sitter (*canguro*).

If you have children who can sit still long enough for a performance, Madrid has a few good picks. The Teatro de Titeres en el Retiro (Puppet Theater in the Retiro) plays in the Retiro Park from October to May on weekends and holidays. Cuarta Pared (Fourth Wall) stages plays for children, and Teatro Lope de Vega often has productions for young audiences. Teatro de la Zarzuela has matinées for kids. If mobility is key, Teleférico runs cable cars out over the Casa de Campo. Pista de Hielo (Ice Rink) offers public skating sessions and figure skating classes.

➤INFORMATION: **Teatro de Titeres en el Retiro** (Parque del Retiro, Retiro). **Cuarta Pared** (Ercilla 17, Centro). **Teatro Lope de Vega** (Gran Vía 57, Centro). **Teatro de la Zarzuela** (Jovellanos 4, Centro). **Teleférico** (Paseo Pintor Rosales s/n, Centro, tel. 91/541–7450), open October–May, weekends noon–8, June–September, daily 11–8. **Pista de Hielo** (Agustín de Foxá s/n, Chamartín, tel. 91/315–6308), open Thursday–Friday 5:30–10, weekends 11:30–2 and 5:30–10.

FOOD

Visiting children may turn up their noses at some of Spain's regional specialties. Although kids seldom get their own menus, most restaurants are happy to provide kids with such simple dishes as plain grilled chicken, steak, or fried potatoes. *Pescadito frito* (batter-fried fish) is one Spanish dish that most kids do seem to enjoy. If all else fails, chains like McDonald's, Burger King, and Pizza Hut are well represented the major cities and popular resorts.

SIGHTS AND ATTRACTIONS

Museum admissions and bus and metro rides are generally free for children up to age five. We indicate places that children might especially enjoy with a rubber duck (🦆) in the margin.

SUPPLIES AND EQUIPMENT

Disposable diapers (*pañales*), formula (*leche maternizada*), and bottled baby foods (*papillas*) are readily available at supermarkets and pharmacies.

Computers on the Road

A few of Spain's newer hotels, mainly in the major cities, provide data ports for Internet access in guest rooms. If you need to bring your computer, *see* Electricity. Virtually every town with more than two traffic lights has at least one cybercafé, most with hourly rates under €3.

Customs and Duties

When shopping abroad, **keep receipts** for all purchases. Upon reentering the country, **be ready to show customs officials what you've bought.** If you feel a duty is incorrect, appeal the assessment. If you object to the way your clearance was handled, note the inspector's badge number. In either case, first ask to see a supervisor. If the problem isn't resolved, write to the appropriate authorities, beginning with the port director at your point of entry. European Union residents who have traveled only within the EU need not pass through customs upon returning to their home country. If you plan to come home with large quantities of alcohol or tobacco, check EU limits beforehand.

From countries that are not part of the European Union, visitors age 15 and over may *enter* Spain duty-free with up to 200 cigarettes or 50 cigars, up to 1 liter of alcohol over 22 proof, and up to 2 liters of wine. Dogs and cats are admitted as long as they have up-to-date vaccination records from their home country.

IN AUSTRALIA

Australian residents who are 18 or older may bring home A$400 worth of souvenirs and gifts (including jewelry), 250 cigarettes or 250 grams of tobacco, and 1,125 ml of alcohol (including wine, beer, and spirits). Residents under 18 may bring back A$200 worth of goods. Prohibited items include meat products. Seeds, plants, and fruits need to be declared upon arrival.

►INFORMATION: **Australian Customs Service** (Regional Director, Box 8, Sydney, NSW 2001, tel. 02/9213–2000 or 1300/ 363263; 1800/020504 quarantine-inquiry line, fax 02/9213– 4043, www.customs.gov.au).

IN CANADA

Canadian residents who have been out of Canada for at least seven days may bring in C$750 worth of goods duty-free. If you've been away fewer than seven days but more than 48 hours, the duty-free allowance drops to C$200. If your trip lasts 24 to 48 hours, the allowance is C$50. You may not pool allowances with family members. Goods claimed under the C$750 exemption may follow you by mail; those claimed under the lesser exemptions must accompany you. Alcohol and tobacco products may be included in the seven-day and 48-hour exemptions but not in the 24-hour exemption. If you meet the age requirements of the province or territory through which you reenter Canada, you may bring in, duty-free, 1.5 liters of wine or 1.14 liters (40 imperial ounces) of liquor or 24 12-ounce cans or bottles of beer or ale. If you are 19 or older you may bring in, duty-free, 200 cigarettes and 50 cigars. Check ahead of time with the Canada Customs and Revenue Agency or the Department of Agriculture for policies regarding meat products, seeds, plants, and fruits. You may send an unlimited number of gifts (only one gift per recipient, however) worth up to C$60 each duty-free to Canada. Label the package UNSOLICITED GIFT— VALUE UNDER $60. Alcohol and tobacco are excluded.

➤INFORMATION: **Canada Customs and Revenue Agency** (2265 St. Laurent Blvd. S, Ottawa, Ontario K1G 4K3, tel. 204/983–3500, 506/636–5064, or 800/461–9999, www.ccra-adrc.gc.ca/).

IN NEW ZEALAND

All homeward-bound residents may bring back NZ$700 worth of souvenirs and gifts; passengers may not pool their allowances, and children can claim only the concession on goods intended for their own use. For those 17 or older, the duty-free allowance also includes 4.5 liters of wine or beer; one 1,125-ml bottle of spirits; and either 200 cigarettes, 250 grams of tobacco, 50 cigars, or a combination of the three up to 250 grams. Meat products, seeds, plants, and fruits must be declared upon arrival to the Agricultural Services Department.

➤INFORMATION: **New Zealand Customs** (Head office: The Customhouse, 17–21 Whitmore St., Box 2218, Wellington, tel. 09/300–5399 or 0800/428–786, www.customs.govt.nz).

IN THE U.K.

If you are a U.K. resident and your journey was wholly within the European Union, you probably won't have to pass through customs when you return to the United Kingdom. If you plan to bring back large quantities of alcohol or tobacco, check EU limits beforehand. In most cases, if you bring back more than 200 cigars, 800 cigarettes, 10 liters of spirits, and/or 90 liters of wine, you have to declare the goods upon return.

➤INFORMATION: **HM Customs and Excise** (Portcullis House, 21 Cowbridge Rd. E, Cardiff CF11 9SS, tel. 029/2038–6423 or 0845/010–9000, www.hmce.gov.uk).

IN THE U.S.

U.S. residents who have been out of the country for at least 48 hours may bring home, for personal use, $400 worth of foreign goods duty-free, as long as they haven't used the $400 allowance or any part of it in the past 30 days. This exemption may include 1 liter of alcohol (for travelers 21 and older), 200 cigarettes, and 100 non-Cuban cigars. Family members from the same household who are traveling together may pool their $400 personal exemptions. For fewer than 48 hours, the duty-free allowance drops to $200, which may include 50 cigarettes, 10 non-Cuban cigars, and 150 milliliters of alcohol (or perfume containing alcohol). The $200 allowance cannot be combined with other individuals' exemptions, and if you exceed it, the full value of all the goods will be taxed. Antiques, which the U.S. Customs Service defines as objects more than 100 years old, enter duty-free, as do original works of art done entirely by hand, including paintings, drawings, and sculptures.

You may also send packages home duty-free, with a limit of one parcel per addressee per day (except alcohol or tobacco products or perfume worth more than $5). You can mail up to $200 worth of goods for personal use; label the package PERSONAL USE and attach a list of its contents and their retail value. If the package contains your used personal belongings, mark it PERSONAL GOODS RETURNED to avoid paying duties. You may send up to $100 worth of goods as a gift; mark the package UNSOLICITED GIFT. Mailed items do not affect your duty-free allowance on your return.

➤**INFORMATION: U.S. Customs Service** (for inquiries, 1300 Pennsylvania Ave. NW, Washington, DC 20229, tel. 202/354–1000, www.customs.gov; for complaints, Customer Satisfaction Unit, 1300 Pennsylvania Ave. NW, Room 5.5A, Washington, DC 20229; for registration of equipment, Office of Passenger Programs, 1300 Pennsylvania Ave. NW, Room 5.4D, Washington, DC 20229, tel. 202/927–0530).

Dining

The restaurants included in this book are the cream of the crop in each price range.

HEALTH CONCERNS

At the end of 2000, the first cases of bovine spongiform encephalopathy (BSE, or "mad cow disease") were detected among Spanish cattle, raising questions about the safety of eating beef in Spain. Cattle is subject to testing, and local health authorities have declared it safe to eat Spanish beef and veal, but dishes containing brains or cuts including the spinal cord should be avoided.

Disabilities and Accessibility

Unfortunately, Spain has made only modest strides in making traveling easy for visitors with disabilities. The Prado and some newer museums, like Madrid's Reina Sofía and Thyssen-Bornemisza, have wheelchair-accessible entrances or elevators. Most of the churches, castles, and monasteries on a sightseer's itinerary involve a lot of walking, often on uneven terrain.

Electricity

To use electric equipment from the United States, **bring a converter and adapter.** Spain's electrical current is 220 volts, 50 cycles alternating current (AC); wall outlets take Continental-type plugs, with two round prongs. If your appliances are dual-voltage you'll need only an adapter. Don't use 110-volt outlets, marked FOR SHAVERS ONLY, for high-wattage appliances such as hair dryers. Most laptop computers operate equally well on 110 and 220 volts, so they require only an adapter.

Embassies

➤IN MADRID: **Australia** (Plaza Descubridor Diegos de Ordas 3, tel. 91/441–9300). **Canada** (Calle Nuñez de Balboa 35, tel. 91/423–3250). **New Zealand** (Plaza Lealtad 2, tel. 91/523–0226). **United Kingdom** (C. Fernando el Santo 16, tel. 91/319–0200). **United States** (C. Serrano 75, tel. 91/587–2200).

Emergencies

In any emergency, call 112. Emergency pharmacies are required to be open 24 hours a day on a rotating basis; pharmacy windows and the major daily newspapers list pharmacies open round-the-clock that day.

➤**DOCTORS AND DENTISTS: English-speaking-doctor referrals** (Conde de Aranda 7, Salamanca, tel. 91/435–1823).

➤**EMERGENCY SERVICES: Ambulancias Cruz Roja** (Red Cross Ambulances; tel. 91/522–2222) are on call 24 hours a day. **Ambulancias SAMUR** (Red Cross Ambulances; tel. 092) are always available.

➤**HOSPITALS: Hospital La Paz** (Paseo de la Castellana 261, Chamartín, tel. 91/358–2600). **Hospital Ramon y Cajal** (Carretera de Colmenar, Km 9, Chamartín, tel. 91/336–8000). **Hospital 12 de Octubre** (Carretera de Andalucía, Km 5.4, Carabanchel, tel. 91/390–8000).

Etiquette and Behavior

The Spanish are very tolerant of foreigners and their different ways, but you should always behave with courtesy. Be respectful when visiting churches: casual dress is fine if it's not gaudy or unkempt. Spaniards do object to men going bare-chested anywhere other than the beach or poolside and generally do not look kindly on public displays of drunkenness. When addressing Spaniards with whom you are not well acquainted, use the formal *usted* rather than the familiar *tu*. For more on language, *see* Language.

BUSINESS ETIQUETTE

Spanish office hours can be confusing to the uninitiated. Some offices stay open more or less continuously from 9 to 3, with a very short lunch break. Others open in the morning, break up the day with a long lunch break of two–three hours, then reopen at 4 or 5 until 7 or 8. Spaniards enjoy a certain notoriety for their lack of punctuality, but this has changed dramatically in recent years: you are expected to show up for meetings on time. Smart dress is the norm.

Spaniards in international fields tend to conduct business with foreigners in English. If you speak Spanish, address new colleagues with the formal *usted* and the corresponding verb conjugations, then follow the lead in switching to the familiar *tu* once a working relationship has been established.

Gay and Lesbian Travel

Since the end of Franco's dictatorship, the situation for gays and lesbians in Spain has improved dramatically: the paragraph in the Spanish civil code that made homosexuality a crime was repealed in 1978. Violence against gays does occur, but it's generally restricted to the rougher areas of very large cities.

➤**LOCAL RESOURCES: Gai Inform** (Fuencarral 37, 28004 Madrid, tel. 91/523–0070).

Health

Sunburn and sunstroke are real risks in summertime Spain. On the hottest sunny days, even those who are not normally bothered by strong sun should cover themselves up; carry sunblock lotion; drink plenty of fluids; and limit sun time for the first few days. Medical care is good in Spain, but nursing is perfunctory, as relatives are expected to stop by and look after inpatients' needs. Spain was recently documented as having the highest number of AIDS cases in Europe. Those applying for work permits will be asked for proof of HIV-negative status.

FOOD AND DRINK

The major health risk in Spain is *diarrea*, or traveler's diarrhea, caused by eating contaminated fruit or vegetables or drinking contaminated water. So **watch what you eat.** Avoid ice, uncooked food, and unpasteurized milk and milk products, and **drink only bottled water** or water that has been boiled for several minutes, even when brushing your teeth. Mild cases may respond to Imodium (known generically as loperamide) or Pepto-Bismol, both of which can be purchased over the counter. In Spain, ask for *un antidiarreico*, which is the general term for antidiarrheal medicine; Fortasec is a well-known brand. You don't need a doctor's prescription to buy it. Drink plenty of purified water or tea—chamomile (*manzanilla*) is a good folk remedy. In severe cases, rehydrate yourself with a salt-sugar solution (½ teaspoon salt (*sal*) and 4 tablespoons sugar (*azúcar* per quart of water).

OVER-THE-COUNTER REMEDIES

Over-the-counter remedies are available at any *farmacia* (pharmacy), recognizable by the large green crosses outside. Some will look familiar, such as *aspirina* (aspirin), while other medications are sold under various brand names. If you regularly take a nonprescription medicine, take a sample box or bottle with you, and the Spanish pharmacist will provide you with its local equivalent.

Holidays

Spain's national holidays include January 1, January 6 (Epiphany), Good Friday, Easter, May 1 (May Day), August 15 (Assumption), October 12 (National Day), November 1 (All Saints'), December 6 (Constitution), December 8 (Immaculate Conception), and December 25.

In addition, each region, city, and town has its own holidays honoring political events and patron saints. Madrid holidays include May 2 (Madrid Day), May 15 (St. Isidro), and November 9 (Almudena).

If a public holiday falls on a Tuesday or Thursday, remember that **many businesses also close on the nearest Monday or Friday** for a long weekend called a *puente* (bridge). If a major holiday falls on a Sunday, businesses close on Monday.

Language

Fortunately, Spanish is fairly easy to pick up, and your efforts to speak it will be graciously received. Learn at least a few basic phrases, *see* the Spanish Vocabulary at the end of this guide.

If your Spanish breaks down, you should have no trouble finding people who speak English in major cities and coastal resorts, but you won't necessarily be able to count on the bus driver or the passerby on the street. Those who do speak English may speak the British variety, so don't be surprised if you're told to queue (line up) or take the lift (elevator) to the loo (toilet). Many guided tours at museums and historic sites are in Spanish; ask about the language that will be spoken before you sign up.

Lodging

By law, hotel prices must be posted at the reception desk and should indicate whether or not the value-added tax (IVA; 7%) is included. Breakfast is normally *not* included. Note that high-season rates prevail not only in summer but also during Holy Week and local fiestas. The lodgings we review are the cream of the crop in each price category. We always list the facilities available, but we don't specify whether they cost extra; so when pricing accommodations, always ask what's included and what's not.

Madrid B&B arranges short-term lodging in private apartments, some hosted and some unhosted.

➤CONTACT: **Madrid B&B** (437 J St., Suite 210, San Diego, CA 92101, tel. 800/872–2632; 619/531–1179 in the U.S.; fax 619/531–1686; www.madridbandb.com).

Mail and Shipping

Madrid's main post office, the Palacio de Comunicaciones, is at the intersection of Paseo de Recoletos and Calle de Alcalá, just one long block north of the Prado Museum. There are also innumerable Internet cafés and services throughout the city. Amiweb Cyber and Cybershop Vortex offer faxing, printing, scanning, and e-mail connections. Ask shopkeepers and bartenders for the nearest on-line venue.

➤POST OFFICE: **Palacio de Comunicaciones** (Plaza de Cibeles s/n, Centro, tel. 91/396–2443), open weekdays 8 AM–10 PM, Saturday 8:30–2, and Sunday 10–1.

➤INTERNET CAFÉS: **Amiweb Cyber** (Gran Vía 80, 6th floor, office 612, Centro), open weekdays 10 AM–midnight, weekends 11 AM–midnight. **Cybershop Vortex** (Ave María 20, Centro), open daily 10 AM–midnight.

OVERNIGHT SERVICES

When time is of the essence, or when you're sending valuable items or documents overseas, you can use a courier (*mensajero*). The major international agencies, such as Federal Express and UPS, have representatives in Spain; the biggest Spanish courier service is Seur. MRW is another local courier that provides express delivery worldwide.

➤MAJOR SERVICES: **DHL** (tel. 902/122424). **Federal Express** (tel. 900/100871). **MRW** (tel. 900/300400). **Seur** (tel. 902/101010). **UPS** (tel. 900/102410).

POSTAL RATES

Airmail letters to the United States and Canada cost €.75 up to 20 grams. Letters to the United Kingdom and other EU countries cost €.50 up to 20 grams. Letters within Spain are €.25. Postcards carry the same rates as letters. You can buy stamps at post offices and at licensed tobacco shops.

Metro Travel

The metro is quick, frequent, and, at €1 no matter how far you travel, cheap. Even cheaper is the 10-ride Metrobus ticket, or *billete de diez*, which costs €5, is also valid for buses, and is accepted by automatic turnstiles (lines at ticket booths can be long). The system is open from 6 AM to 1:30 AM, though a few entrances close earlier. There are 10 metro lines, and system maps in stations detail their color-coded routes. Note the end station of the line you need, and follow signs to the correct corridor. Exits are marked SALIDA.

Money Matters

Spain is no longer a budget destination, but prices still compare slightly favorably with those elsewhere in Europe. Coffee in a bar generally costs €.75 (standing) or €.90 (seated). Beer in a bar: €.95 standing, €1 seated. Small glass of wine in a bar: around €1. Soft drink: €1–€1.20 a bottle. Ham-and-cheese sandwich: €1.80–€2.70. Two-kilometer (1-mi) taxi ride: €2.40, but the meter keeps ticking in traffic jams. Local bus or subway ride: €.81–€1.20. Movie ticket: €3–€4.80. Foreign newspaper: €1.80. In this book we quote prices for adults only, but note that **children, students, and senior citizens almost always pay reduced fees.** For information on taxes in Spain, *see* Taxes.

➤**REPORTING LOST CARDS: American Express** (tel. 900/941413). **Diners Club** (tel. 901/101011). **MasterCard** (tel. 900/974445). **Visa** (tel. 900/971231).

CURRENCY

On January 1, 2002, the European monetary unit, the Euro (€), went into circulation in Spain and the other countries that have adopted it (Austria, Belgium, Finland, France, Germany, Greece, Ireland, Italy, Luxembourg, the Netherlands, and Portugal). Euro notes come in denominations of 5, 10, 20, 50, 100, 200, and 500; coins are worth 1 cent of a Euro, 2 cents, 5 cents, 10 cents, 20 cents, 50 cents, 1 Euro, and 2 Euros. At press time, exchange rates were favorable for most English-speaking travelers: €.94 to the U.S. dollar, €.65 to the pound sterling, €1.45 to the Canadian dollar, €1.66 to the Australian dollar, €1.93 to the New Zealand dollar, and €9.39 to the South African rand.

CURRENCY EXCHANGE

For the most favorable rates, **change money through banks.** Although ATM transaction fees may be higher abroad than at home, ATM rates are excellent because they are based on wholesale rates offered only by major banks. You won't do as well at exchange booths in airports or rail and bus stations, in hotels, in restaurants, or in stores. To avoid lines at airport exchange booths, **convert some money before you leave home.**

Packing

Pack light. Although baggage carts are free and plentiful in most Spanish airports, they're rare in train and bus stations.

On the whole, Spaniards dress up more than Americans or the British. Summer is hot nearly everywhere; visits in winter, fall, and spring call for warm clothing and, in winter, boots. It makes sense to wear casual, comfortable clothing and shoes for sightseeing, but you'll want to **dress up a bit in large cities, especially for fine restaurants and nightclubs.** American tourists are easily spotted for their sneakers—if you want to blend in, wear leather shoes. On the beach, anything goes; it's common to see females of all ages wearing only bikini bottoms, and many of the more remote beaches allow nude sunbathing. Regardless of your style, **bring a cover-up** to wear over your bathing suit when you leave the beach.

In luggage to be checked, **never pack prescription drugs or valuables.** To avoid customs and security delays, carry medications in their original packaging. Don't pack any sharp objects in your carry-on luggage, including knives of any size or material, scissors, manicure tools, and corkscrews, or anything else that might arouse suspicion.

CHECKING LUGGAGE

You are allowed one carry-on bag and one personal article, such as a purse or a laptop computer. Make sure that everything you carry aboard will fit under your seat or in the overhead bin. Get to the gate early, so you can board as soon as possible, before the overhead bins fill up.

Passports and Visas

When traveling internationally, **carry your passport** even if you don't need one (it's always the best form of I.D.) and **make two photocopies of the data page** (one for someone at home and another for you, carried separately from your passport). If you lose your passport, promptly call the nearest embassy or consulate and the local police.

ENTERING SPAIN

Visitors from the United States, Australia, Canada, New Zealand, and the United Kingdom need a valid passport to enter Spain. Australians who wish to stay longer than a month also need a visa, available from the Spanish embassy in Canberra.

Safety

Petty crime is a huge problem in Spain's most popular tourist destinations. The most frequent offenses are pickpocketing (particularly in Madrid and Barcelona) and theft from cars (all over the country). **Never, ever leave anything valuable in a parked car,** no matter how friendly the area feels, how quickly you'll return, or how invisible the item seems once you lock it in the trunk. Thieves can spot rental cars a mile away, and they work very efficiently. In airports, laptop computers are choice prey. When walking the streets, particularly in large cities, carry your cash (and/or traveler's checks, ATM, or credit cards) in a money belt that is securely tied around your waist and hidden under your clothes. Men should carry their wallet in the front pocket; women who need to carry purses should strap them across the front of their bodies. Leave the rest of your valuables in the safe at your hotel. On the beach, in cafés and restaurants (particularly in the well-touristed areas), and in Internet centers, always keep your belongings on your lap or tied to your person in some way. Additionally, be cautious of any odd or unnecessary human contact, verbal or physical, whether it's a tap on the shoulder, someone spilling their drink at your table, and so on. Thieves often work in twos, so while one is attracting your attention, the other could be swiping your wallet.

WOMEN IN SPAIN

The traditional Spanish custom of the *piropo* (a shouted "compliment" to women walking down the street) is fast disappearing, though women traveling alone may still encounter it on occasion. The piropo is harmless, if annoying, and should simply be ignored.

Taxes

VALUE-ADDED TAX

Value-added tax, similar to sales tax, is called IVA in Spain (pronounced "*ee-vah*"; for *impuesto sobre el valor añadido*). It is levied on both products and services such as hotel rooms and restaurant meals. When in doubt about whether tax is included, ask, "*Está incluido el IVA*"?

The IVA rate for hotels and restaurants is 7%, regardless of their number of stars or forks. A special tax law for the Canary Islands allows hotels and restaurants there to charge 4% IVA. Menus will generally say at the bottom whether tax is included (IVA *incluido*) or not (*más* 7% IVA).

Whereas food, pharmaceuticals, and household items are taxed at the lowest rate, most consumer goods are taxed at 16%. A number of shops, particularly large stores and boutiques in holiday resorts, participate in Global Refund (formerly Europe Tax-Free Shopping), a VAT refund service that makes getting your money back relatively hassle-free. On purchases of more than €90, you're entitled to a refund of the 16% tax. **Ask for the Global Refund form** (called a Shopping Cheque) in participating stores. You show your passport and fill out the form; the vendor then mails you the refund, or—often more convenient—you **present your original receipt to the VAT office at the airport** when you leave Spain. (In both Madrid and Barcelona, the office is near the duty-free shops. Save time for this process, as lines can be long.) Customs signs the original and refunds your money on the spot in cash (Euros) or sends it to the central office to process a credit-card refund. Credit-card refunds take a few weeks.

➤**VAT REFUNDS: Global Refund** (99 Main St., Suite 307, Nyack, NY 10960, tel. 800/566–9828, www.globalrefund.com).

Taxis

Taxis are one of Madrid's few truly good deals. Meters start at €2 and add €.75 per kilometer (½ mi) thereafter (€1 per kilometer at night, on weekends and holidays, and beyond city limits). Numerous supplemental charges, however, mean that your total cost often bears little resemblance to what you see on the meter. Supplemental charges—over and above your fare—include €1 on Sundays and holidays and between 11 PM and 6 AM, €1 to sports stadiums or the bullring, and €3 (plus €.30 per suitcase) to or from the airport.

Taxi stands are numerous, and taxis are easily hailed in the street—except when it rains, at which point they're exceedingly hard to come by. Available cabs display a LIBRE sign during the day, a green light at night. Spaniards do not tip cabbies, but if you're inspired, €.5 is about right for shorter rides; you can go as high as 10% for a trip to the airport. You can call a cab through Tele-Taxi, Radioteléfono Taxi, or Radio Taxi Gremial.

➤TAXIS AND SHUTTLES: Radio Taxi Gremial (tel. 91/447–5180). Radioteléfono Taxi (tel. 91/547–8200). Tele-Taxi (tel. 91/371–2131).

Telephones

Spain's phone system is perfectly efficient. Direct dialing is the norm. The main operator is Telefónica. Note that only cell phones conforming to the European GSM standard will work in Spain.

AREA AND COUNTRY CODES
The country code for Spain is 34. Phoning home: country codes are 1 for the United States and Canada, 44 for the United Kingdom, 61 for Australia, and 64 for New Zealand.

DIRECTORY AND OPERATOR ASSISTANCE
For general information in Spain, dial 1003. International operators, who generally speak English, are at 025.

INTERNATIONAL CALLS
International calls are awkward from coin-operated pay phones because of the many coins needed; and they can be expensive from hotels, as the hotel often adds a hefty surcharge. Your best bet is to use a public phone that accepts phone cards (☞ Phone Cards) or go to the local telephone office, the *locutorio*: every town has one, and major cities have several. The locutorios near the center of town are generally more expensive; farther from the center, the rates are sometimes as much as one-third less. You converse in a quiet, private booth, and you're charged according to the meter. If the call ends up costing around €3 or more, you can usually pay with Visa or MasterCard.

To make an international call yourself, dial 00, then the country code, then the area code and number.

Madrid's main telephone office is at Gran Vía 28. There's another at the main post office, and a third at Paseo Recoletos 43, just off Plaza Colón. In Barcelona you can phone overseas from the office at Carrer de Fontanella 4, off Plaça de Catalunya.

Before you leave home, **find out your long-distance company's access code in Spain.**

LOCAL CALLS

All area codes begin with a 9. To call within Spain—even locally—dial the area code first. Numbers preceded by a 900 code are toll-free; those starting with a 6 are going to a cellular phone. Note that calls to cell phones are significantly more expensive than calls to regular phones.

LONG-DISTANCE SERVICES

AT&T, MCI, and Sprint access codes make calling long distance relatively convenient, but you may find the local access number blocked in many hotel rooms. First ask the hotel operator to connect you. If the hotel operator can't comply, ask for an international operator, or dial the international operator yourself.

➤**ACCESS CODES IN SPAIN: AT&T** (tel. 900/990011). **MCI** (tel. 900/990014). **Sprint** (tel. 900/990013).

PHONE CARDS

To use a newer pay phone you need a special phone card (*tarjeta telefónica*), which you can buy at any tobacco shop or newsstand, in various denominations. Some such phones also accept credit cards, but phone cards are more reliable.

Time

Spain is on Central European Time, one hour ahead of Greenwich Mean Time, six hours ahead of Eastern Standard Time. Like the rest of the European Union, Spain switches to daylight saving time on the last weekend in March and switches back on the last weekend in October.

Tipping

Waiters and other service staff expect to be tipped, and you can be sure that your contribution will be appreciated. On the other hand, if you experience bad or surly service, don't feel obligated to leave a tip.

Restaurant checks almost always include a service charge, which is not the same as a voluntary tip. **Do not tip more than 10% of the bill,** and leave less if you eat tapas or sandwiches at a bar—just enough to round out the bill to the nearest €1. Tip cocktail servers €.30–€.50 a drink, depending on the bar.

Tip taxi drivers about 10% of the total fare, plus a supplement for a long ride or extra help with luggage. Note that rides from airports carry an official surcharge plus a small handling fee for each piece of luggage.

Tip hotel porters €.50 a bag, and the bearer of room service €.50. A doorman who calls a taxi for you gets €.50. If you stay in a hotel for more than two nights, tip the maid about €.50 per night. The concierge should receive a tip for any additional help he or she provides.

Tour guides should be tipped about €2, ushers in theaters or at bullfights €.15–€.20, barbers €.50, and women's hairdressers at least €1 for a wash and style. Rest-room attendants are tipped €.15.

Tours and Packages

Because everything is prearranged on a prepackaged tour or independent vacation, you spend less time planning—and often get it all at a good price.

BOOKING WITH AN AGENT

Travel agents are excellent resources. But it's a good idea to collect brochures from several agencies, as some agents' suggestions may be influenced by relationships with tour and package firms that reward them for volume sales. If you have a special interest, **find an agent with expertise in that area**; ASTA (☞ Travel Agencies) has a database of specialists worldwide.

Make sure your travel agent knows the accommodations and other services of the place being recommended. Ask about the hotel's location, room size, beds, and whether it has a pool, room service, or programs for children, if you care about these. Has your agent been there in person or sent others whom you can contact? Do some homework on your own, too: local tourism boards can provide information about lesser-known and small-niche operators, some of which may sell only direct.

BUYER BEWARE

Each year consumers are stranded or lose their money when tour operators—even large ones with excellent reputations—go out of business. So **check out the operator**. Ask several travel agents about its reputation, and try to **book with a company that has a consumer-protection program**. (Look for information in the company's brochure.) In the United States, members of the National Tour Association and the United States Tour Operators Association are required to set aside funds to cover your payments and travel arrangements in the event that the company defaults. It's also a good idea to choose a company that participates in the American Society of Travel Agents' Tour Operator Program (TOP); ASTA will act as mediator in any disputes between you and your tour operator.

Remember that the more your package or tour includes the better you can predict the ultimate cost of your vacation. Make sure you know exactly what is covered, and **beware of hidden costs**. Are taxes, tips, and transfers included? Entertainment and excursions? These can add up.

➤**TOUR-OPERATOR RECOMMENDATIONS: American Society of Travel Agents** (☞ Travel Agencies). **National Tour**

Association (NTA; 546 E. Main St., Lexington, KY 40508, tel. 859/226–4444 or 800/682–8886, www.ntaonline.com). **United States Tour Operators Association** (USTOA; 342 Madison Ave., Suite 1522, New York, NY 10173, tel. 212/599–6599 or 800/468–7862, www.ustoa.com).

SIGHTSEEING TOURS

Your hotel can arrange standard city tours in either English or Spanish; most offer Madrid Artístico (including the Royal Palace and the Prado), Madrid Panorámico (a basic half-day tour), Madrid de Noche (including a flamenco or nightclub show), and the Sunday-only Panorámico y Toros (a brief city overview followed by a bullfight). The Plaza Mayor tourist office leads tours of Madrid's old quarters in English every Saturday morning, departing from the office at 10. The same office has a leaflet detailing the popular Spanish-language bus and walking tours run by the *ayuntamiento* (city hall) under the rubric "Descubre Madrid"; you then buy tickets at the Patronato de Turismo. The walking tours depart most mornings; theme options include "Medicine in Madrid," "Goya's Madrid," and "Commerce and Finance in Madrid." For day trips to sites outside Madrid, such as Toledo, El Escorial, and Segovia, contact Julià Tours.

Trapsatur runs the Madrid Visión tourist bus, which makes a 1½-hour circuit of the city with recorded commentary in English. No reservation is needed; just show up at Gran Vía 32 or the front of the Prado Museum. Buses depart every 1¼ hours beginning at 12:30 Monday–Saturday, 10:30 on Sunday. A round-trip ticket costs €8; a day pass, which allows you to get on and off at various attractions, is €13. An identical hop-on, hop-off service on an open-top double decker is operated by Sol Pentours, whose daily 1½-hour tours leave every half hour from Plaza de España, in front of the Crowne Plaza Hotel, between 10 AM and 8 PM. The fare is €9. Contact the Asociación Profesional de Informadores to hire a personal guide.

►CONTACTS: **Asociación Profesional de Informadores** (C. Ferraz 82, Moncloa, tel. 91/542–1214 or 91/541–1221). **Ayuntamiento** (City Hall; C. Mayor 69, Centro, tel. 91/588–2900). **Julià Tours** (Gran Vía 68, Centro, tel. 91/559–9605). **Patronato de Turismo** (C. Mayor 69, Centro, tel. 91/588–2900). **Plaza Mayor tourist office** (Plaza Mayor 3, Centro tel. 91/588–2900). **Sol Pentours** (Gran Vía 26, Centro, tel. 902/303903). **Trapsatur** (tel. 91/302–6039).

Train Travel

For train schedules and reservations, go to any of Madrid's major train stations, visit a travel agent, or call RENFE toll-free. You can charge tickets to your credit card and even have them delivered to your hotel. Madrid has three main train stations: Chamartín, Atocha, and Norte, the last primarily for commuter trains. Remember to confirm which station you need when arranging a trip. Generally speaking, Chamartín, near the northern tip of Paseo de la Castellana, serves points north and west, including Barcelona, San Sebastián, Burgos, León, Oviedo, La Coruña, and Salamanca, as well as France and Portugal. Atocha, at the southern end of Paseo del Prado, serves towns near Madrid, including El Escorial, Segovia, and Toledo, and southern and eastern cities such as Seville, Málaga, Córdoba, Valencia, and Castellón. Atocha also sends AVE (high-speed) trains to Córdoba and Seville.

You can buy train tickets in advance at the train station, which is what most Spaniards do. The lines can be long, so give yourself plenty of time if you plan on buying same-day tickets. For popular train routes, you will need to reserve tickets more than a few days in advance; call RENFE to inquire. The ticket clerks at the stations rarely speak English, so if you need need help or advice in planning a more complex train journey you may be better off going to a travel agency that displays the blue-and-yellow RENFE sign. The price is the same. For shorter, regional train trips, you can often buy your tickets directly from machines in the main train stations. Note that if your itinerary is set in stone and has little room for error, you can buy RENFE tickets through Rail Europe before you leave home.

Commuter trains and most long-distance trains forbid smoking, though some long-distance trains have smoking cars.

➤**TRAIN INFORMATION: Estación de Atocha** (tel. 91/328–9020). **Estación Chamartín** (tel. 91/315–9976). **RENFE** (tel. 902/240202, www.renfe.es/ingles).

Travel Agencies

Scattered throughout Madrid, travel agencies are generally the best way to get tickets, cheap deals, and information without hassles. Madrid & Beyond is a British-run agency that can make all your travel and lodging arrangements in Madrid, other historic cities, and some lovely rural areas.

A good travel agent puts your needs first. Look for an agency that has been in business at least five years, emphasizes customer service, and has someone on staff who specializes in your destination. In addition, **make sure the agency belongs to a professional trade organization.** The American Society of Travel Agents (ASTA)—the largest and most influential in the field with more than 24,000 members in some 140 countries—maintains and enforces a strict code of ethics and will step in to help mediate any agent-client disputes involving ASTA members if necessary. ASTA (whose motto is "Without a travel agent, you're on your own") also maintains a Web site that includes a directory of agents. (If a travel agency is also acting as your tour operator, *see* Buyer Beware in Tours and Packages.)

➤**IN MADRID: American Express** (Plaza de las Cortés 2, tel. 91/322–5500). **Carlson Wagons-Lits** (Paseo de la Castellana 96, tel. 91/563–1202). **Madrid & Beyond** (Gran Vía 59-8D, tel.

91/758–0063, fax 91/542–4391). **Pullmantur** (Plaza de Oriente 8, tel. 91/541–1807).

➤**LOCAL AGENT REFERRALS: American Society of Travel Agents** (ASTA; 1101 King St., Suite 200, Alexandria, VA 22314, tel. 800/965–2782 24-hr hot line, fax 703/739–3268, www. astanet.com). **Association of British Travel Agents** (68–71 Newman St., London W1T 3AH, tel. 020/7637–2444, fax 020/ 7637–0713, www.abtanet.com). **Association of Canadian Travel Agents** (130 Albert St., Suite 1705, Ottawa, Ontario K1P 5G4, tel. 613/237–3657, fax 613/237–7052, www.acta.ca). **Australian Federation of Travel Agents** (Level 3, 309 Pitt St., Sydney, NSW 2000, tel. 02/9264–3299, fax 02/9264–1085, www.afta.com.au). **Travel Agents' Association of New Zealand** (Level 5, Tourism and Travel House, 79 Boulcott St., Box 1888, Wellington 6001, tel. 04/499–0104, fax 04/499–0827, www.taanz.org.nz).

Visitor Information

Madrid has four regional tourist offices. The best is at Duque de Medinaceli 2 (near the Westin Palace), open weekdays 9–7 and Saturday 9–1. The others are at Barajas Airport, open weekdays 9–7 and Saturday 9:30–1:30; the Chamartín train station, open weekdays 8–8 and Saturday 9–1; and the remote Mercado de la Puerta de Toledo, open weekdays 9–7 and Saturday 9–1. The city tourist office on the Plaza Mayor is good for little save a few pamphlets; it's open weekdays 10–8, Saturday 10–2, and Sunday 10–2.

➤**CITY TOURIST OFFICE: Plaza Mayor 3** (tel. 91/588–1636).

➤**REGIONAL TOURIST OFFICES: Duque de Medinaceli 2** (tel. 91/429–4951). **Barajas** (tel. 91/305–8656). **Chamartín** (tel. 91/ 315–9976). **Mercado de la Puerta de Toledo** (Glorieta Puerta de Toledo, 3rd floor, Lavapiés, tel. 91/364–1876).

Web Sites

Do check out the World Wide Web when planning your trip. Be sure to **visit Fodors.com** (www.fodors.com), a complete travel-planning site.

For more information on Spain, visit the Tourist Office of Spain at www.tourspain.es and see www.okspain.es, www.cyberspain.com, or www.red2000.com/spain. For a virtual brochure on Spain's paradors, go to www.parador.es.

When to Go

May and October are the optimal times to come to Spain, as the weather is generally warm and dry. May gives you more hours of daylight, while October offers a chance to enjoy the harvest season, which is especially colorful in the wine regions.

Spain is the number-one destination for European travelers, so **if you want to avoid crowds, come before June or after September.** Crowds and prices increase in the summer, especially along the coasts, as the Mediterranean is usually too cold for swimming the rest of the year, and beach season on the Atlantic coast is shorter still. Spaniards vacation in August, and their migration to the beach causes huge traffic jams on August 1 and 31. Major cities are relaxed and empty for the duration; small shops and some restaurants shut down for the entire month, but museums remain open.

CLIMATE

Summers in Spain are hot: temperatures frequently hit 100°F (38°C), and air-conditioning is not widespread. That said, warm summer nights are among Spain's quiet pleasures.

Winters in Spain are mild and rainy along the coasts, especially in Galicia. Elsewhere, winter blows bitterly cold. Snow is infrequent except in the mountains, where you can ski from December to

March in the Pyrenees and other resorts near Granada, Madrid, and Burgos.

➤FORECASTS: **Weather Channel Connection** (tel. 900/932–8437), 95¢ per minute from a Touch-Tone phone.

The following are average daily maximum and minimum temperatures for Madrid.

MADRID

Jan.	48F	9C	**May**	70F	21C	**Sept.**	77F	25C
	36	2		50	10		57	14
Feb.	52F	11C	**June**	81F	27C	**Oct.**	66F	19C
	36	2		59	15		50	10
Mar.	59F	15C	**July**	88F	31C	**Nov.**	55F	13C
	41	5		63	17		41	5
Apr.	64F	18C	**Aug.**	86F	30C	**Dec.**	48F	9C
	45	7		63	17		36	2

SPANISH VOCABULARY

Basics

ENGLISH	SPANISH	PRONUNCIATION
Yes/no	Sí/no	see/no
Please	Por favor	pohr fah-vohr
May I?	¿Me permite?	meh pehr-mee-teh
Thank you (very much)	(Muchas) gracias	(moo-chas) grah-see-as
You're welcome	De nada	deh nah-dah
Excuse me	Con permiso/perdón	con pehr-mee-so/pehr-dohn
Pardon me/what did you say?	¿Perdón?/Mande?	pehr-dohn/mahn-deh
Could you tell me . . . ?	¿Podría decirme . . . ?	po-dree-ah deh-seer-meh
I'm sorry	Lo siento	lo see-en-to
Good morning!	¡Buenos días!	bway-nohs dee-ahs
Good afternoon!	¡Buenas tardes!	bway-nahs tar-dess
Good evening!	¡Buenas noches!	bway-nahs no-chess
Goodbye!	¡Adiós!/¡Hasta luego!	ah-dee-ohss/ah-stah-lwe-go
Mr./Mrs.	Señor/Señora	sen-yor/sen-yohr-ah
Miss	Señorita	sen-yo-ree-tah
Pleased to meet you	Mucho gusto	moo-cho goose-to
How are you?	¿Cómo está usted?	ko-mo es-tah oo-sted
Very well, thank you.	Muy bien, gracias.	moo-ee bee-en, grah-see-as
And you?	¿Y usted?	ee oos-ted
Hello (on the phone)	Diga	dee-gah

Numbers

1	un, uno	oon, oo-no
2	dos	dohs
3	tres	tress
4	cuatro	kwah-tro
5	cinco	sink-oh
6	seis	saice
7	siete	see-et-eh
8	ocho	o-cho
9	nueve	new-eh-veh
10	diez	dee-es
11	once	ohn-seh
12	doce	doh-seh
13	trece	treh-seh
14	catorce	ka-tohr-seh
15	quince	keen-seh
16	dieciséis	dee-es-ee-saice
17	diecisiete	dee-es-ee-see-et-eh
18	dieciocho	dee-es-ee-o-cho
19	diecinueve	dee-es-ee-new-ev-eh
20	veinte	vain-teh
21	veinte y uno/ veintiuno	vain-te-oo-noh
30	treinta	train-tah
32	treinta y dos	train-tay-dohs
40	cuarenta	kwah-ren-tah
50	cincuenta	seen-kwen-tah
60	sesenta	sess-en-tah
70	setenta	set-en-tah
80	ochenta	oh-chen-tah
90	noventa	no-ven-tah
100	cien	see-en
200	doscientos	doh-see-en-tohss
500	quinientos	keen-yen-tohss
1,000	mil	meel
2,000	dos mil	dohs meel

Days of the Week

Sunday	domingo	doh-meen-goh
Monday	lunes	loo-ness
Tuesday	martes	mahr-tess
Wednesday	miércoles	me-air-koh-less
Thursday	jueves	hoo-ev-ess
Friday	viernes	vee-air-ness
Saturday	sábado	sah-bah-doh

Useful Phrases

Do you speak English?	¿Habla usted inglés?	ah-blah oos-ted in-glehs
I don't speak Spanish	No hablo español	no ah-bloh es-pahn-yol
I don't understand (you)	No entiendo	no en-tee-en-doh
I understand (you)	Entiendo	en-tee-en-doh
I don't know	No sé	no seh
I am American/ British	Soy americano (americana)/ inglés(a)	soy ah-meh-ree-kah-no (ah-meh-ree-kah-nah)/in-glehs(ah)
My name is . . .	Me llamo . . .	meh yah-moh
Yes, please/ No, thank you	Sí, por favor/ No, gracias	see pohr fah-vor/ no grah-see-ahs
Yesterday/today/ tomorrow	Ayer/hoy/mañana	ah-yehr/oy/mahn-yah-nah
This morning/ afternoon	Esta mañana/tarde	es-tah mahn-yah-nah/tar-deh
Tonight	Esta noche	es-tah no-cheh
This/Next week	Esta semana/ la semana que entra	es-tah seh-mah-nah/lah seh-mah-nah keh en-trah
This/Next month	Este mes/el próximo mes	es-teh mehs/el prok-see-moh mehs
How?	¿Cómo?	koh-mo
When?	¿Cuándo?	kwahn-doh
What?	¿Qué?	keh
What is this?	¿Qué es esto?	keh es es-toh

Why?	¿Por qué?	por keh
Who?	¿Quién?	kee-yen
Where is . . . ?	¿Dónde está . . . ?	dohn-deh es-tah
the train station?	la estación del tren?	la es-tah-see-on del train
the subway station?	la estación del metro?	la es-ta-see-on del meh-tro
the bus stop?	la parada del autobus?	la pah-rah-dah del oh-toh-boos
the bank?	el banco?	el bahn-koh
the hotel?	el hotel?	el oh-tel
the post office?	la oficina de correos?	la oh-fee-see-nah deh-koh-reh-os
the museum?	el museo?	el moo-seh-oh
the hospital?	el hospital?	el ohss-pee-tal
the bathroom?	el baño?	el bahn-yoh
Here/there	Aquí/allá	ah-key/ah-yah
Open/closed	Abierto/cerrado	ah-bee-er-toh/ser-ah-doh
Left/right	Izquierda/derecha	iss-key-er-dah/dare-eh-chah
Straight ahead	Todo recto	toh-doh-rec-toh
Is it near/far?	¿Está cerca/lejos?	es-tah sehr-kah/leh-hoss
I'd like . . .	Quisiera . . .	kee-see-ehr-ah
a room	una habitación	oo-nah ah-bee-tah-see-on
the key	la llave	lah yah-veh
a newspaper	un periódico	oon pehr-ee-oh-dee-koh
a stamp	un sello	say-oh
How much is this?	¿Cuánto cuesta?	kwahn-toh kwes-tah
A little/a lot	Un poquito/mucho	oon poh-kee-toh/moo-choh
More/less	Más/menos	mahss/men-ohss
I am ill	Estoy enfermo(a)	es-toy en-fehr-moh(mah)
Please call a doctor	Por favor llame un medico	pohr fah-vor ya-meh oon med-ee-koh
Help!	¡Ayuda!	ah-yoo-dah

On the Road

Avenue	Avenida	ah-ven-ee-dah
Broad, tree-lined boulevard	Paseo	pah-seh-oh
Highway	Carretera	car-reh-ter-ah
Port; mountain pass	Puerto	poo-ehr-toh
Street	Calle	cah-yeh
Waterfront promenade	Paseo marítimo	pah-seh-oh mahr-ee-tee-moh

In Town

Cathedral	Catedral	cah-teh-dral
Church	Iglesia	tem-plo/ee-glehs-see-ah
City hall, town hall	Ayuntamiento	ah-yoon-tah-me-yen-toh
Door, gate	Puerta	poo-ehr-tah
Main square	Plaza Mayor	plah-thah mah-yohr
Market	Mercado	mer-kah-doh
Neighborhood	Barrio	bahr-ree-o
Tavern, rustic restaurant	Mesón	meh-sohn
Traffic circle, roundabout	Glorieta	glor-ee-eh-tah
Wine cellar, wine bar, wine shop	Bodega	boh-deh-gah

Dining Out

A bottle of . . .	Una bottella de . . .	oo-nah bo-teh-yah deh
A glass of . . .	Un vaso de . . .	oon vah-so deh
Bill/check	La cuenta	lah kwen-tah
Breakfast	El desayuno	el deh-sah-yoon-oh
Dinner	La cena	lah seh-nah
Menu of the day	Menú del día	meh-noo del dee-ah
Fork	El tenedor	ehl ten-eh-dor
Is the tip	¿Está incluida la	es-tah in-cloo-ee-dah

included?	propina?	lah pro-pee-nah
Knife	El cuchillo	el koo-chee-yo
Large portion of tapas	Ración	rah-see-ohn
Lunch	La comida	lah koh-mee-dah
Menu	La carta, el menú	lah cart-ah, el meh-noo
Napkin	La servilleta	lah sehr-vee-yet-ah
Please give me . . .	Por favor déme . . .	pohr fah-vor deh-meh
Spoon	Una cuchara	oo-nah koo-chah-rah

index

Fodor's
Key to the Guides

America's guidebook leader publishes guides for every kind of traveler. Check out our many series and find your perfect match.

Fodor's Gold Guides
America's favorite travel-guide series offers the most detailed insider reviews of hotels, restaurants, and attractions in all price ranges, plus great background information, smart tips, and useful maps.

Fodor's Road Guide USA
Big guides for a big country—the most comprehensive guides to America's roads, packed with places to stay, eat, and play across the U.S.A. Just right for road warriors, family vacationers, and cross-country trekkers.

COMPASS AMERICAN GUIDES
Stunning guides from top local writers and photographers, with gorgeous photos, literary excerpts, and colorful anecdotes. A must-have for culture mavens, history buffs, and new residents.

Fodor's CITYPACKS
Concise city coverage with a foldout map. The right choice for urban travelers who want everything under one cover.

Fodor's EXPLORING GUIDES
Hundreds of color photos bring your destination to life. Lively stories lend insight into the culture, history, and people.

Fodor's POCKET GUIDES
For travelers who need only the essentials. The best of Fodor's in pocket-size packages for just $9.95.

Fodor's To Go
Credit-card–size, magnetized color microguides that fit in the palm of your hand—perfect for "stealth" travelers or as gifts.

Fodor's FLASHMAPS
Every resident's map guide. 60 easy-to-follow maps of public transit, parks, museums, zip codes, and more.

Fodor's CITYGUIDES
Sourcebooks for living in the city: Thousands of in-the-know listings for restaurants, shops, sports, nightlife, and other city resources.

Fodor's AROUND THE CITY WITH KIDS
68 great ideas for family days, recommended by resident parents. Perfect for exploring in your own backyard or on the road.

Fodor's ESCAPES
Fill your trip with once-in-a-lifetime experiences, from ballooning in Chianti to overnighting in the Moroccan desert. These full-color dream books point the way.

Fodor's FYI
Get tips from the pros on planning the perfect trip. Learn how to pack, fly hassle-free, plan a honeymoon or cruise, stay healthy on the road, and travel with your baby.

Fodor's Languages for Travelers
Practice the local language before hitting the road. Available in phrase books, cassette sets, and CD sets.

Karen Brown's Guides
Engaging guides to the most charming inns and B&Bs in the U.S.A. and Europe, with easy-to-follow inn-to-inn itineraries.

Baedeker's Guides
Comprehensive guides, trusted since 1829, packed with A–Z reviews and star ratings.

FODOR'S POCKET MADRID

EDITORS: Carissa Bluestone, Paul Eisenberg

Editorial Contributors: George Semler, AnneLise Sorenson

Editorial Production: Kristin Milavec

Maps: David Lindroth, *cartographer;* Bob Blake and Rebecca Baer, *map editors*

Design: Fabrizio La Rocca, *creative director;* Tigist Getachew, *art director;* Jolie Novak, *senior picture editor;* Melanie Marin, *photo editor*

Production/Manufacturing: Colleen Ziemba

Cover Photo: Ricardo Ordoñez/Age Fotostock America

COPYRIGHT

Third Edition

ISBN 1–4000–1102–7

ISSN 1531–3409

IMPORTANT TIP

Although all prices, opening times, and other details in this book are based on information supplied to us at press time, changes occur all the time in the travel world, and Fodor's cannot accept responsibility for facts that become outdated or for inadvertent errors or omissions. So **always confirm information when it matters,** especially if you're making a detour to visit a specific place.

SPECIAL SALES

PRINTED IN THE UNITED STATES OF AMERICA

10 9 8 7 6 5 4 3 2 1